WALCH PUBLISHING

D1710642

Daily Warm-Ups

DAILY EDITS

Hannah Jones

Level I

The classroom teacher may reproduce materials in this book for classroom use only.
The reproduction of any part for an entire school or school system is strictly prohibited.
No part of this publication may be transmitted, stored, or recorded in any form
without written permission from the publisher.

1   2   3   4   5   6   7   8   9   10

ISBN 0-8251-5456-1
Copyright © 2005
J. Weston Walch, Publisher
P.O. Box 658 • Portland, Maine 04104-0658
walch.com

Printed in the United States of America

The *Daily Warm-Ups* series is a wonderful way to turn extra classroom minutes into valuable learning time. The 180 quick activities—one for each day of the school year—offer students practice in revising and editing. These daily activities may be used at the very beginning of class to get students into learning mode, near the end of class to make good educational use of that transitional time, in the middle of class to shift gears between lessons—or whenever else you have minutes that now go unused. In addition to providing students with structure and focus, they are a natural path to other language arts activities.

Daily Warm-Ups are easy-to-use reproducibles—simply photocopy the day's activity and distribute it. Or make a transparency of the activity and project it on the board. You may want to use the activities for extra credit points or as a method of prompting classroom discussion.

However you choose to use them, *Daily Warm-Ups* are a convenient and useful supplement to your regular lesson plans. Make every minute of your class time count!

Daily Warm-Ups: Daily Edits

Find ten capitalization errors and five spelling errors in the letter below. Rewrite the letter with the errors corrected.

september 2, 20__

deer Student,

Welcom to my Class and to Charlotte Cove middle school. Like you, i'm looking forward to an Exiting year togehter.

To help me get to know you, please write a letter telling me a bit about Yourself. Hand in final draft by next tuesday.

sinserely,

Mr. Klepp

Correct the fifteen errors in this passage.

I sure hope this guy isn't wierd, Pete thought, as he stared wistfully out the window of his classroom down to the soccer feild below. Mr. Klepp sure *looked* a bit off—he had a scrufy mushtache that covered his upper lip, and his shirt was butoned wrong. He smiles and gestured like a maniac. And, worst of all, assigned homework on the first day.

But their were hopeful signs, to. Pictures of classic rock stars hung on his walls. They're were inspiring sayings on the wall, too, such as, "Give piece a chance," by john lennon. *Maybe this guy is a hipie*, Pete thought. At least that would be interesting.

As Mr. Klepp dismissed the class, Pete begins to daydream about what he would say in his letter.

2

Daily Warm-Ups: Daily Edits

Rewrite Samantha's letter to Mr. Klepp, substituting more precise vocabulary for the underlined words.

September 4, 20__

Dear Mr. Klepp,

I'm <u>happy</u> to be in your class this year. You seem like a <u>nice</u> teacher because you explain things <u>well</u> and treat everyone <u>well</u>.

You asked for some information about me, and here it is. I <u>like</u> language arts. In fact, it is my favorite subject. I <u>want</u> to be a novelist when I grow up, so writing <u>well</u> is important to me. I also <u>like</u> working to save the environment because it makes me feel <u>good</u>.

I dislike <u>bad</u> teachers who don't explain things <u>well</u> and who give lots of homework. I hope you're not one of them. I also <u>don't like</u> cafeteria food, as I am a vegetarian and they rarely serve <u>good</u> food.

Yours truly,

Samantha

Daily Warm-Ups: Daily Edits

This passage is composed entirely of simple sentences. Rewrite it so that it has more sentence variety. Also correct the five spelling errors.

So far Charlotte Cove Middle School is pretty good. I like having a different teacher for each class. I like moving around during the day. I love having allied arts. We have a lot more freedum here. It's cool to have kids from different schools all together. I am making new friends. Some of them live in town. Some of them are from the country.

There are some problems with middle school. I can't seem to remember the right books for my clases. I forget my locker combination. I still get lost sometimes. It takes me a long time to get from class to class. The teachers are pretty strick. They assine allot of homework. The bus ride to school is much longer. I'd still rather be in middle school than in elementary school, though.

4

Edit Pete's letter to Mr. Klepp. Mark your corrections on the letter.

September 2, 20___

Dear Mr. Klepp,

you can see from the date of this letter that I am no procrastinating on my homework. Usually I wate until the last minute but am real excited to tell you about myself.

I can see from your posters that you like rock music. I been playing guitar for two years, and I'm looking for a band to join. My goal is to be a working musician when I grow up right now I just want to meet some kids and play some music.

Language arts isn't my best subject I like to rite songs but not poetry. I can ryme pretty good, though this summer I wrote a song about my cat I had to rhyme *fur ball* with something. I worked on it for hours, until I came up with *snow squall*. Ill play it for you, if you want.

Yours,

Pete

5

Add quotation marks to this conversation between Pete and his big buddy, Leo. Put a paragraph symbol (¶) everywhere there should be a new paragraph.

Hey, are you Pete? Leo asked, tapping him on the shoulder. Pete turned around defensively. Yeah, he said, What do you want? Pete was feeling paranoid about the older kids after stories he'd heard of practical jokes. Leo answered, I'm your big buddy. Mr. Klepp asked me to show you around school because we're both musicians. Really? What do you play? Are you in a band? What grade are you in? Pete had suddenly lost his shyness. Um, let me see if I can remember all your questions, Leo replied. I'm in eighth grade. I play drums in a band called Truck Stop, and we play everything—rock, pop, punk, reggae, you name it. And we're looking for a guitarist who can write songs. At that, Pete was speechless.

Substitute similes and metaphors for the underlined phrases to add drama to the story. Write your substitutions above the phrases you are replacing.

Isabel's cheeks were <u>very red</u> as she pulled her rolling backpack down the hall. It had seemed like such a good idea when she and her mom had gone school shopping, but now the backpack seemed <u>out of place</u>. Everyone else had normal backpacks, the kind you wear on your back. Isabel heard a few students laughing at her as the wheels rolled noisily down the corridor. She felt everyone's eyes <u>on her</u>. Even her best friend, Samantha, was staring at her.

Desperate, Isabel dragged Samantha into a corner. "Do I look <u>stupid</u> with this <u>thing</u>?" she wailed.

"No, silly," Samantha replied. "I was just thinking that my books <u>are very heavy</u>. I would love to have a backpack like yours."

7

Proofread the following memorandum from Principal Eisner about the dress code. Pay special attention to punctuation (colons and commas) and capitalization. Mark your corrections on the memo.

TO   parents and students of Charlotte cove Middle school

FROM principal Perez

DATE   september 15 20___

SUBJECT dress code

It has come to my attention that some of our students are not following the Dress Code at the Middle School. The following articles of clothing are not allowed at our school flip-flops, T-shirts with offensive language, clothing that exposes the midriff, ripped or torn clothing, or excessively tight or short pants.

We reserve the right to send home any student who doesn't adhere to the dress code. Please send questions or complaints to this address Principal Perez, c/o dress code committee, charlotte cove middle school, charlotte cove maine 04___.

8

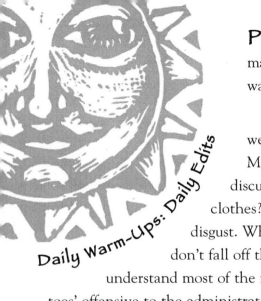

Punctuate the following story. Insert quotation marks where needed, show paragraph breaks using the ¶ symbol, and watch out for apostrophe errors.

Quiet down, please, Mr. Klepp asked, but it was no use. Student's were reading the memo from Principal Perez in disbelief. Look, Mr. Klepp said, rather than complaining pointlessly, lets have a discussion about the memo. Cliff immediately moaned, No ripped clothes? There goes my whole wardrobe. He threw the memo down in disgust. What skater has clothes that arent ripped? he asked. Skater's who don't fall off their boards all the time, Cliff, Mr. Klepp answered. I can understand most of the rule's, Samantha said, but why no flip-flop's? Are my toes' offensive to the administration? Maybe you should ask them, Mr. Klepp replied. For homework, please draft a letter in response to Principal Perezs memo.

9

Write a memo to the principal of Charlotte Cove Middle School in which you agree or disagree with Principal Perez's dress code. Defend your position. Have a partner edit your letter for errors and for the strength of your argument.

Daily Warm-Ups: Daily Edits

10

Edit this story for subject-verb agreement. Be sure that it's written consistently in the past tense. Cross out the five misspelled words and write them correctly.

Tryouts for soccer was after school today, and Pete thought he was going to through up. He knew he was pretty good, but he isn't shure he would be good enough to play with seventh and eighth graders. There was probley going to be only a few precious spaces on the teem.

As he loped out to the field, though, he sees a reassuring sight. His new bandmates, Leo and Nate, was kicking a ball back and fourth on the sidelines.

"Hey," Nate calls. "How are you doing, little man?"

"Fine," he say. "I'd be a lot better if you didn't call me 'little man,' though."

Leo laughs and asked, "Are you nervous?"

"Nah," Pete lied. Just then, his buddy Cliff walked up to them. "Hey, little man, how's it going?" Pete asks, with a big grin on his face.

11

Underline the clichés in this passage. Revise them to sound more original.

On the girls' soccer field, Samantha was trying to convince Isabel that trying out was as easy as pie. Isabel had never played before, but when she got to middle school, she promised herself that she wouldn't be a couch potato. Playing soccer, with her best friend to show her the ropes, had seemed like the perfect solution.

But now soccer balls seemed to be flying everywhere, and everyone else knew what to do. She felt like a fish out of water.

"Sammy," she cried, "I can't do this."

"Sure you can, Izzie," Samantha shouted encouragingly, as she headed a ball to Isabel. It hit her hard on the bridge of the nose.

"Owww! No, I can't," Isabel repeated. "Look at me. You can't teach an old dog new tricks."

"Come on. If at first you don't succeed, try, try again!" Sammy kicked the ball to Isabel, who, getting her second wind, passed Samantha and ran down the field.

"C'mon, Sammy! Let's get this show on the road!" Isabel shouted.

Mr. Klepp is giving his students a required reading list for their language arts class. Correct the list, and be sure to find the five spelling errors. Mark you corrections on the list.

Mr. Klepp's Slitely Abridged List of Best Stories Ever

Short Storys: Harrison Bergeron by Kurt Vonnegut Jr.

the "Gift Of The Magi" By O. Henry

<u>The Lottery</u> by Shirley Jackson

thank you, ma'am by langston Hughes

Novel's: the <u>Chocolate War</u> By Robert Cormier

"The Wiches" by Roald Dahl

The Outsiders by S E Hinton

Alices adventures In Wonderland by Lewis Carroll

13

There are ten incorrect verb forms in this story. Cross them out and correct them.

"Why do we have to read?" Cliff moaned to Mr. Klepp. "I have soccer practice four afternoons a week, and every book I've ever red makes me fall asleep."

Isabel cryed, "I love Roald Dahl, Mr. Klepp. I studied *The Witches* in the fifth grade at my old school! I think it's one of the greatest stories ever wrote."

"Suck up," Cliff whispered.

"Hey, I heard that," Izzie replyed angrily, jumping from her seat. "Look, just because I happen to *like* school doesn't give you the right to . . ."

"Okay, guys, quit it," Mr. Klepp warned. "Isabel, set down. I have an idea," Mr. Klepp continued. "Cliff, why don't you spend recess today learning Isabel how to play soccer, and she can spend tomorrow helping you with *The Witches*? In the meantime, can I get a little peace and quiet so I can teach?"

Cliff glared at Isabel. Isabel sat her book down and begun to cry. It was going to be an interesting couple of days.

14

With a partner, write a short dialogue between Isabel and Cliff, in which he teaches her soccer or she teaches him about *The Witches*. Be sure to use proper dialogue punctuation!

15

Proofread the following poster carefully and mark your corrections.

Attenshun All Students'

Pleese come to the fift annuel halloween soshul!

who, all your freinds in the six, seven, and eight grade

what, an evning of games, ice creme, and local bands

Where, the gymnaseum

When, this friday

Why, to have fun and rase money for the eight grade class

16

Find the errors in the following dialogue. Mark your corrections.

Pete saw a girl he didn't reconize putting up posters in the six grade hallway. "Hey," he asked her shyly, "do you know which bands are playing at the social?"

"Yes, of course," she answered. "The froot loops a band from the high school are playing. Theirs also the Charlotte Cove jazz ensemble a group that the band director started. And my band truck stop is playing."

Pete almost fainted. "Wait, your in truck stop? Im in truck stop!" he exclaimed. "Are you . . . ?"

"Chrissie," she answered, and held out her hand. "I haven't met you because I've been out with mono, and I'm in seventhe grade," she explained. "You must be Pete."

Pete almost forgotten what his name was. Chrissie was real pretty. He smiled like a fool.

"I hear you're wrighting us a song for friday," Chrissie said. "I can't wate to sing it."

"Yeah, sure," Pete answered dazedly, as he walked to language arts.

17

Help Pete write a song for the social about his favorite things. He needs to find vivid similes to describe the things he loves.

1. My cat is like _____

    because_____.

2. My friend Cliff is like_____ because

    _____.

3. My teacher Mr. Klepp is like_____ because

    _____.

4. My soccer team is like _____because _____.

5. My band is like _____ because _____.

Once you have chosen five similes, write a song using them. Or, if you prefer, write a song using similes to describe your own favorite things.

18

Daily Warm-Ups: Daily Edits

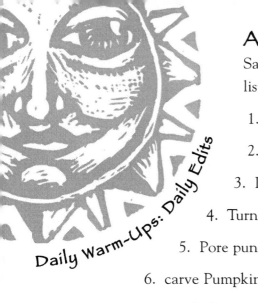

As a member of the Charlotte Cove Student Council, Samantha has to set up the gym for the school social. Proofread the list of instructions. Mark your corrections on the list.

1. Sit 50 chairs around the perimiter of the gym

2. Lie a clothe under the food table to protect the gym floor

3. Put out three hundred paper cups and 400 napkins

4. Turn on the stage lites

5. Pore punch into the punch bole

6. carve Pumpkins for deccorations

7. Bye halloween candy, and put in bowls

8. get change for the cash box

9. Sit out a collection of bored games

10. Open the gym dores, and lets people in!

19

Cliff wrote a review of the bands that performed at the social. Revise the review to eliminate unnecessary wordiness. Mark your corrections on the review.

Last Friday, the Charlotte Cove Middle School recently hosted one of the most exciting, original, and unique music shows in history.

There were three bands that performed, and all of them performed really very well. There was one band that performed that was called Froot Loops that was from the local high school known as Charlotte Cove High School. They played music that was music in the style or genre known as country music, which in my opinion is okay but not really my absolute favorite kind of music.

There was a second band that wowed listeners and fans with its excellent, surprising, and cool blend of jazz and rock, and that was none other than the famous and well-known Jazz Ensemble from our own school.

Finally, there was another band that performed that was from our school, Charlotte Cove Middle School. They were probably the best and most awesome band of all the three bands, which is not only my opinion but also seemed to be the opinion of the crowd, too. They were Truck Stop, and they played a number of hits and very popular ones at that, including an original song by my best friend, Pete.

20

Use the conjunctions in the box to combine the following pairs of simple sentences. Rewrite the new sentences on another sheet of paper.

| although | before | after | since | but | when | if | and | so | because |

1. Isabel was angry. Cliff wrote all over her planner.

2. She went to Mr. Klepp to tell. She decided to ask Cliff why he had done it.

3. Cliff saw the look on Isabel's face. He got worried.

4. He didn't think writing on her planner was a big deal. Obviously, she did.

5. He decided to apologize. She was so upset.

6. Isabel saw how sorry he was. She felt better.

7. She told Cliff she wouldn't tell Mr. Klepp. He promised not to do it again.

8. They shook hands. Isabel went to recess.

9. Cliff was putting on his coat. He saw Sammy's planner.

10. He knew he shouldn't. He got out his markers and wrote on Sammy's planner.

21

© 2005 Walch Publishing

Isabel and Samantha are writing a letter to leave in Cliff's desk. It is filled with run-ons, and there are also seven misspelled words. Rewrite the letter with the corrections made.

Dear (NOT!) Cliff,

We have had it with your writing on are stuff, why do you do it, we never did anything to you.

Unlike you who never writes anything down we actually use our planners to write down important stuff, we write our homework assinements in there and we can't tell what's doo if you scribble all over the pages, also we have privet stuff like our friends' phone numbers and we don't want you getting into them.

We are not going to tell on you this time, we're not babies and we can handle this ourselves but believe us, Cliff, if you do one more thing like this, we will handel it and you won't like it.

Yours truly (NOT!),

Samantha and Isabel

P.S. Just becase you're a looser doesn't mean you have to ruin our lives, too.

22

Correct the errors in the following dialogue. Mark your corrections on the passage.

Cliff showed Pete the note in the hallway. "Can you believe this." He asked? "There such babies, I say we get our revenge."

Pete wasn't sure, he relied on his planner, to, in fact, he was kind of a neat freak, and he had to admit that Cliff was a disorganized slob. Pete also thought it was mean for Cliff to be messing with the girls stuff he didn't want Cliff to think he was a geek.

Pete said "I dont know Cliff, is it really worth getting detention to bother scribbling on a couple of planners?"

"Oh, Im way passed planners now," Cliff answered. "This is all tout war."

23

Take the facts of this story, and write your own version rich with descriptive language and sentence variety.

Cliff sneaked into Mr. Klepp's classroom after school. He told the custodian that he had forgotten his homework. He looked around the classroom for a way to get back at the girls. He saw a stack of tests on Mr. Klepp's desk. Mr. Klepp hadn't corrected them yet. Cliff found Sammy's and Isabel's papers and changed some answers. Now they would fail the test. He also made their answers the same. It looked like they had cheated. Finally, he found his test. He changed some of his answers to what Isabel and Samantha had. Then he left the classroom and went home.

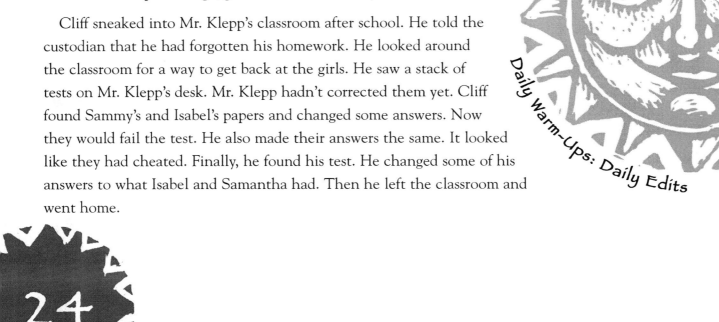

Daily Warm-Ups: Daily Edits

24

Edit the following story. Mark your corrections on the story.

Mr. Klepp was sitting at his kitchen table and grading his students quizzes, he noticed that Pete had brought his grade up from a C to an A–. He corrected Kyles test, noticed that he was still having a hard time keeping dates strait. When he got to Isabels paper he smiled he knew how much knowlege she had on the subject. How much she loved ancient cultures. How many books she had read on the subject.

As he started to grade the paper. He noticed something wierd, some of Isabels answers were in a differnt handriting, the ones in her writing were correct, the ones in the black scribble were rong. He new she new the rite answers. But not what had happened.

Next he got to Sammys paper. Same black scribbles. Same incorrect answers. He recongized that writing, he didn't know who's it was. Until he got to Cliff's paper.

Mr. Klepp was going to need to disipline someone tomarrow but it wasn't the girls.

25

Find the spelling errors in the following dialogue. Mark your corrections.

Mr. Klepp walked into the classroom, set down his briefcase, and announced, "Today I'll be handing back the test ment to assess your knowlege of Ancient Egypt." The hole class looked up expectently. Cliff gave Pete a suttle, triumphent look.

"First," Mr. Klepp continued, "I am going to check the validety of my test. He looked towerd Samantha and Isabel, who were sitting next to each other. "Unfortunately, some students' ansers on this test mached, and it apperes that there was some cheeting. However, I don't want to condem anybody until I know for shore."

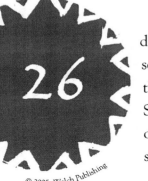

Cliff suddenly looked very uncomfortable. Mr. Klepp said, "Please fold your paper down the middle, and number the first colum one through ten. Then number the second column from eleven to twenty." Mr. Klepp walked down the aisles and checked the students' work. As he read the questions from the test the day before, he saw Samantha and Isabel confidantly writing down the answers. He saw Cliff glancing offen at his nieghbor's paper. Mr. Klepp collected the papers, set them on his desk, and said, "Thank-you. Class dismised. Would Samantha, Isabel, and Cliff please see me?"

26

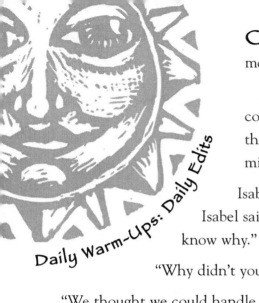

Combine the following simple sentences to make a more interesting story. Rewrite the story with your revisions.

Mr. Klepp asked Cliff to wait in the hallway. He asked the girls to come into his room. They got inside. He told them, "Cliff changed the answers on your tests." He asked them, "Do you know why he might do that?"

Isabel and Samantha looked at Mr. Klepp. They looked at each other. Isabel said, "He has been taking our planners and writing in them. We don't know why."

"Why didn't you tell me?" Mr. Klepp asked.

"We thought we could handle it ourselves," Samantha replied. "We wrote him a letter. We asked him nicely to stop."

"Okay, Mr. Klepp said. "I'm going to see Cliff now. I'm going to get his side of the story."

27

Correct Cliff's written statement. Rewrite the corrected paragraph.

Mr. Klepp its true I did change the answers on Sammy's and Izzie's papers but I did it for a good reason. There snobs, they think they are so smart. I wrote some notes in there planners, I was triing to be freindly. They rote me a lettter. Said I was a looser. Said I don't do my work and am disorganized. Said thed do stuff to me if I did anything again. Maybe trying to be there friends. Wasn't a good idea but I was trying to be nice, I'll never do that again. I get cot becase I'm not as sneeky as they are but there just as bad.

28

Revise this dialogue between Cliff and the girls. Mark your corrections below.

Isabel: If you wanted to be are friends. Why didn't you just talk to us?

Cliff: I thought you would think I was stupid, your both so smart.

Isabel: Writing on our planners didn't exactly make you look like a genius.

Samantha: Besides we don't think you're stupid we think you're cool.

Cliff: you always make fun of me when I say the wrong answer.

Isabel: Sometimes we feel unpopular we make fun of the popular kids because being smart is all we got.

Sammy: Hey we've got each other!

Cliff: Well maybe we can hang out when I get back.

Sammy and Isabel: Where are you going?

Cliff: Mr. Klepp suspended me. For a day. I'm going to the retirement home to volunteer in the cafeteria.

29

Fix the dangling modifiers in the following passage, and correct the five misspelled words. Rewrite the passage with the corrections made.

The steps to the retirement home that Cliff climbed were rickety and old. He thought he could hear voices as he opened the front door that whisperd about him. Walking up to the front desk with shakeing knees and a quivuring voice, he said, "I'm Cliff, checking in for work."

At the age of five, his grandfather had gone into a retirment home. Remembering his grandfather, lying there in his bathrobe and smoking his cigar, Cliff felt frightened to face the patience. The head nurse, Mr. Blythe, reassured Cliff that he would just be serving the residents soup with a smile.

30

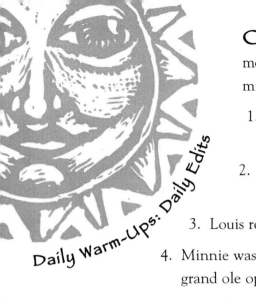

Cliff wrote sentences about some of the people he met at the retirement home. Redraft his sentences to eliminate misplaced modifiers and fix capitalization errors.

1. Bernice was a woman during world war II who had helped to build aircraft carriers while raising a family.

2. A man called Grant had flown a crop duster in his twenties all over the midwest.

3. Louis remembered migrating from oklahoma to the west in the dust bowl.

4. Minnie was a vaudeville star in a dance number who had performed at the grand ole opry.

5. A couple named Mr. and Mrs. Suzuki had been placed in an internment camp by the U.S. government who were Japanese-American during world war II.

31

Proofread this interview between Samantha and a resident of the Sunnyside Retirement Home.

Samantha: What was life like during the great depression?

Mr. Wilson: We was very poor, Sammy. All of the people I knew was poor. At first my mother, father, and me traveled around the country looking for work, but then my dad got a job building bridges for president Roosevelt's wpa project, a government program to give we depression-era families some relief.

Samantha: Did you have a job?

Mr. Wilson: All of us worked. My brothers and me did chores around the house and worked in the garden. My mother raised we kids, kept the house, and cooked all the food for my brothers and I.

Daily Warm-Ups: Daily Edits

32

Proofread this interview between Isabel and her great-grandmother.

Isabel: Where did you grow up, Grammie?

Grammie: We lived on the lower east side of manhattan, in new york city.

Isabel: Describe your appartment.

Grammie: We lived in a tenement house. We had to climb four flights of stairs to get to our place, and there wasn't no hot water. Everybody hanged laundry out the windows, so walking down my alley was like being under a circus tent. My grandparents, who had emigrated from russia, lived in the apartment below us, and my mother's sister and her family lived next door. My life was filled with family.

Isabel: What did your father do?

Grammie: He worked on the railroad as a pullman porter. My mother worked for the bell telephone company as one of the first operators.

33

Proofread this interview between Pete and his great-grandfather.

Pete: What did you do for work during the 'thirties?

Gramp: I was a guitar player in a hawaian band.

Pete: Are you *kidding*? Thats so cool!

Gramp: Yes, we was pretty cool. My band and me traveled all around new england in our model t ford. We gave concerts, offering lessons, and even doing radio advertisements.

Pete: Wait, I thought you said you lived in hawaii

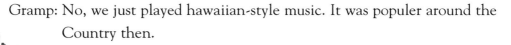

Gramp: No, we just played hawaiian-style music. It was populer around the Country then.

Daily Warm-Ups: Daily Edits

34

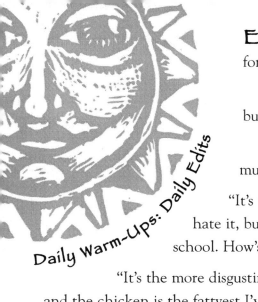

Edit the dialogue below. Pay attention to spelling, verb forms, and forms of modifiers. Mark your corrections below.

Peter and Cliff were in the cafateria. Pete brung lunch from home, but Cliff buyed a school lunch. They were compairing their meals.

"Hey Pete, how's the liverwurst?" Cliff asked, looking over at Pete's mushey bread and smelley cold cuts.

"It's the worse lunch my mom makes," Pete complained. "She knows I hate it, but she thinks the proteen will make me the intelligentest kid at school. How's your lunch?" Pete asked.

"It's the more disgusting food I've ever eaten. The peas are the mushyest and the chicken is the fattyest I've ever had. The pudding is the lumpyest on the planet."

"Look at how many kids waist their food here," Pete said. "We should start a petishun to get better food."

"Yeah," Cliff agreed, "and we should ask for someone who can cook good, too."

35

Correct the spelling and dialogue punctuation in the following story.

Cliff and Pete walked into Mr. Klepp's classroom to complain about their lunches. They noticed that he was eating a beautiful green and purple salid with bright red tomatos, yello peppers, and crustey crootons in it. He also had some lovly hard-boyled eggs in the salad.

Hey, where did you get that? Pete asked.

I made it Mr. Klepp answered.

What do you mean, Cliff asked, Did you go to the salad bar at the store and put it together?

No, Mr. Klepp answered, I made it. I grew the vegitables in my garden, I raised the chickins that layed the eggs in my backyard.

Oh, the boys said. That sounds like a lot of work.

Not if you love it, Mr. Klepp replyed. Would you boys like to see my gardin?

Field trip to Mr. Klepp's house! the boys shouted, as the rest of the class came in from lunch.

36

Change this story from the passive voice to the active voice and eliminate unnecessary wordiness. Rewrite the revised story below.

Excitement was felt by the children as their bus was driven up the dirt road to Mr. Klepp's house by the bus driver. Actually, it seemed more like a farm than a house. One of the things that was different about Mr. Klepp's house was that it had one side that had been made from glass. "That is my greenhouse, class," the students were told by Mr. Klepp. "Vegetables are started there early in the spring, and I can even have tropical fruit in the long, cold Maine winters when I keep my fruit trees in there." Another thing that was different about the house was that instead of a backyard with grass, vegetables had been planted by Mr. Klepp. The students were taken back to the garden, and fresh vegetables were picked by each of the students for a huge salad, which was served to them at lunch.

37

Find the errors in this story. Mark your corrections below.

As Mr. Klepps students munched on there salad and a crusty loaf of bread that Mr. Klepp had baked that weekend, Sammy seen something out the window that make her jump. "Mr. Klepp!" she screemed, "Their is a giant white chicken running around in you're backyard!"

"Thats not a chicken," Mr. Klepp laffed between bites of salad. "That's a goose. Her eggs are in the quiche your eating right now."

"Im going to be sick," Isabel said.

In the meantime, Sammy was out of her chair and runing to the backyard to meet this adorable duck. Mr. Klepp called, "Wate!" but it was to late. No sooner had Sammy started chaseing the goose than the goose turns around, honkeing like a lunatic, and started chasing Sammy!

38

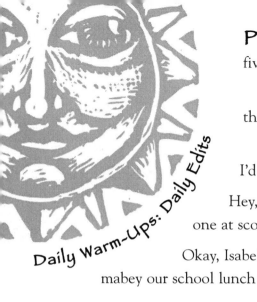

Punctuate the class dialogue, and correct the five misspelled words.

Thanks for takeing us to your farm, I mean house, Cliff said when they got back to class. I think that was the best food I've ever eatin.

Me, too, Sammy added. It was cool to see where food comes from. I'd never pulled a carrot from the ground before, or picked lettuce.

Hey, Pete said. If you can have a farm in your yard, why can't we have one at scool?

Okay, Isabel said. We could give the vegetables and eggs to the cafeteria, and mabey our school lunch would taste better.

Well, Mr. Klepp said, I do teach biology in the sixth grade. He thought for a moment. Yes, I think it's a great idea! he said. But it will cost money to get the supplies. We'll have to do some fund-raising.

39

Write a letter to the principal of Charlotte Cove Middle School, requesting money to build a greenhouse and to buy supplies for a class garden. Trade letters with a partner, and edit each other's work for strength of argument, spelling, and mechanics.

Daily Warm-Ups: Daily Edits

40

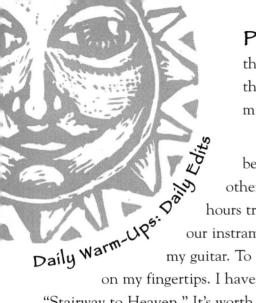

Paragraphs should develop one main idea. Read the following paragraph. Underline the topic sentence, and cross out the sentence that doesn't belong. Find and correct the five misspelled words.

I belong to a band called Truck Stop. Being in a band isn't easy, because for every minuet on stage, you have to spend an hour doing other stuff. My band reherses after school three days a week. We spend hours trying to line up gigs to play. Every one of us spends time caring for our instraments, and in my case I had to mow lawns for six months to afford my guitar. To learn how to play, I practiced for so many hours that I got blisturs on my fingertips. I have a dog named Chico that howls every time I play "Stairway to Heaven." It's worth all the time and effort though, because being in a band is grate.

41

Write a topic sentence for each of the following paragraphs. Correct the five errors in each.

First, take two pieces of bred and lie them on a plate. Second, take a knife and scoop two tablespoons of peanut butter out of the jar. Third, spred the peanut butter onto one of the slices of bread. Forth, with a spoon, scoop out about two tablespoons of jelly. Fifth, spread the jelly on the other piece of bread. Finally, lay one slice of bread on top of the other, with the jelly side faceing the peanut butter side.

Topic sentence: _____

The sky was getting dark in the middle of the day. Huge clowds were boiling up on the horizon. A feirce wind started to blow from the west. All the leafs blew upside down. The smell of thunder filled the air, and my dog hided under the bed, whimpering. My mom walked around the house, shutting windows and unpluging the computer and television.

Topic sentence: _____

42

Underline the topic sentence in the following paragraph. Cross out the sentence that doesn't belong. Find and correct the five spelling errors.

Mr. Klepp's classroom is unlike most sixth-grade classrooms. For instance, Mr. Klepp's students write poems to the vegetables they grow in their class garden. When they study ecosystums, they use their own garden to look at food webs. They sit around watching their food scraps get eaten by worms, and then they put the composte into their vegetable patch. They even have a class pet, a duck named LuLu. I went to school years ago in a small town in Ohio. To learn how to write effectivly, they send real letters to their principle about changes theyd like to make in their school.

43

Here are a main idea and three supporting ideas. Put them into your own words to write a paragraph. Underline your topic sentence.

Main idea: School is harder than adults think.

Supporting idea: Students study many subjects during the day.

Supporting idea: They have to adapt to many teachers' different teaching styles.

Supporting idea: They have homework, club meetings, and sports at the end of the day.

Combine the simple sentences to add variety to the story. Correct the five misspelled words. Rewrite the story with your revisions below.

Pete was practicing with his band. They were getting frusterated. They had been playing the same song for two hours. Pete couldn't get the guitar part right. He felt really stupid. He was supposed to be thinking about getting the cords right on the song. Instead he was thinking about the others. He was wondering if they thought he was too young. He was wondering if they regreted inviting him into the band. He was wondering if Chrissie liked him.

Leo said, "Let's try one more time from the top." The band began playing. A sound like a dieing cat came from Pete's guitar. He got really mad. He used every ounce of his self-control to set his guitar down gently. He walked out of Leo's garage. His head was down. His cheeks were burning with shame. He was triing not to cry.

45

Put commas where they are needed in the following story. Correct the five misspelled words.

"I wounder what's wrong with Pete" Nate said.

"I don't know" Leo answered "but I'll find out." He laid his drumsticks down and headed for Pete's tree house which Leo knew was his favorate place to go when he was feeling upset.

As he rode his bike up to Pete's house he saw Marjorie Pete's mom mowing the front lawn. "Have you seen Pete? He left practice without saying goodby" Leo explained.

"I didn't notice him come in Leo" she said. "I've had the lawn mower going full blast and I must not have heared him."

"I'll check in the tree house" Leo said but Marjorie had started the lawn mower again and couldn't hear him.

46

There are ten pairs of commonly confused words in the following story. Circle the correct one of the two.

Leo found Pete up in his tree house. "Hey, are you (alright/all right)?" Leo asked.

"Of (coarse/course) I'm okay," Pete grumbled. "I just made a complete idiot of myself." Pete lowered his eyes, and Leo looked away, pretending he didn't (hear/here) Pete crying.

"Why do you think (your/you're) an idiot?" Leo asked. "We were all having trouble with the song. And you have the hardest part, playing (lead/led) guitar."

"I don't know," Pete said. "(It's/Its) hard to explain, but being in the band makes me feel really cool and like a (looser/loser) at the same time. I brag to all my sixth-grade friends, but (than/then) I go to practice and feel like a big (waist/waste) of time around you guys."

"If you weren't cool, you wouldn't be in the band," Leo reassured Pete.

"Does everybody feel that way? Even Chrissie?" Pete asked.

Suddenly, it was (plain/plane) to Leo why Pete was so upset.

47

© 2005 Walch Publishing

Cross out the ten commonly misspelled words. Write the correct word above the misspelled word.

Pete was having a horrible nightmare. The band was altogether again, and they were already to play the song. Pete said, "Can't we take a five-minute brake?" His mouth was as dry as a dessert, and his face shown with sweat.

"Sure, we can take five," Chrissie said. "I need some piece and quite after you're horrible playing." Suddenly, she seemed to look right threw him. "And you need a shower," she said, holding her nose. "You wreak."

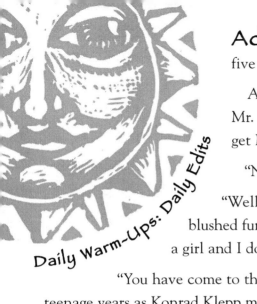

Add commas to the following story. Correct the five misspelled words.

As the other students left for lunch Pete stayed behind to talk to Mr. Klepp who was erasing the bored. Pete cleared his throat hoping to get Mr. Klepp's attention. "Um Mr. Klepp are you busy?" Pete asked.

"No of coarse not" Mr. Klepp answered. "What's on you're mind?"

"Well I was wondering if you've ever liked a girl." Pete stopped and blushed furiously. "I mean I'm sure you've liked a girl but the thing is I like a girl and I don't know what to do about it."

"You have come to the right place" Mr. Klepp said. "I was known in my teenage years as Konrad Klepp most desperate kid at Morse High."

"What did you do about it?" Pete asked although he was afraid to hear the answer.

"I did what any self-respecting guitarist would do" Mr. Klepp answered. "I wrote her a song."

"Wow that's brillient" Pete said. On the way to recess he grabed his notebook and a pen.

49

Here's a simple description of Chrissie. Use this information to write similes and metaphors for Pete to use in a song about her. Write Pete's song in the space below.

1. Chrissie has long, black hair.

   Simile: Your hair is as _____ as_____.

2. Her eyes are green

   Simile: Your eyes are like _____.

3. Her skin is smooth.

   Metaphor: Your skin _____.

50

4. Her laugh sounds musical.

   Simile: Your laugh is like _____.

5. She is kind and caring.

   Metaphor: Your heart _____.

Add commas, semicolons, and question marks to the following story. Correct the five misspellings.

Pete arrived at school ten minutes early he had arranged to meet Mr. Klepp to play him his song about Chrissie he didn't want anybody else to here him. When he arrived at the classroom Mr. Klepp was at his desk eating a huge bowl of something wierd.

"What is that stuff" Pete asked.

"It's granola, yogurt, and fruit" Mr. Klepp answered. "Do you want to try it"

"Uh no thanks" Pete answered "I brought you my song do you want to hear it"

"Does a dog yelp when someone steps on its foot" Mr. Klepp replied somewhat strangely as usual Pete ignored the question.

"Okay here goes" Pete began. He cleared his throat got out his guitar and sang "Oooooh Chrissie/ you're so pritty/ you got lips like rubies/ and skin like a baby" Pete looked up and asked "Is that good so far"

"Excellant" Mr. Klepp answered his eyes were twinkling mischeivously though and Pete wondered if he really liked it.

51

Add punctuation and capitalization to the following letter.

november 15 20___

dear truck stop members

the eighth-grade class is planning a dance to be held on the friday before thanksgiving break and we were wondering if you would play we know it's short notice but you were the favorite band at the social earlier this year and we would really like to have you as our band

the class would be willing to pay you twenty percent of the money we earn we are going to sell tickets for five dollars so you would earn a dollar for everyone who comes to the dance you would need to play between 700 and 1000 PM and you would need to set up and strike your equipment that evening

please let us know if you are willing to play thank-you for considering our offer

sincerely

claire fields

eighth-grade class president

52

Revise the following story. Correct the punctuation and capitalization. Correct the misspelled words.

When Pete got to band practice. He saw his friends gathered around a letter. They had there head's together and they were talking quietly for a minuet Pete thought they were talking about him. Chrissie looked up and saw Pete she said, "Oh my gosh, Pete. Look at this!" She ran over to him holding the letter and jumping up and down. Handed him the letter and when he was finished reading she gave him a big hug. "Isn't it great" she asked.

"Yeah, it's great" Pete replied he tucked the lyrics of his new song in his back pocket thinking that he'd like to suprise her with his new song at the dance.

53

Correct the verbs in this note, left in Pete's tree house, and correct the misspelled words.

Hey Pete,

I have came to see you every day this week, and you hasn't been here. I been calling you every night, but I guess you didn't got your messages because you never calls me back. I don't know if you is angry with me. If you are, you don't have no good reason. I haven't done nothing to you.

All of your friends is beginning to think you don't like them. They saying Pete is to good to hang out with sixth-graders, now that he in a band. If you don't want them to think that, than you pay attention to your real friends, like me.

Sighned,

Cliff

54

The following long paragraph is really about two different ideas. Break the paragraph in two, and put each of the sentences into the appropriate paragraph. Make sure each paragraph has a topic sentence. Rewrite the revised paragraphs.

The Northeast has four distinct seasons: winter, spring, summer, and autumn. During the New England winter, temperatures drop, and there is often snow. Rivers and lakes turn to ice, but the ocean is too large and too salty to freeze. The days are short, and the nights are long. Some people prefer to live in a climate that is more consistent. For them, the Southwest is an ideal setting. During the northeastern spring, the days lengthen, buds appear on the trees, and the whole world seems to come to life. Although there are definitely seasonal changes in the Southwest, temperatures are dependably warm during the day and cool at night. Summers in the Northeast are warm and dry. Summer is the main growing season of the Northeast. In autumn, temperatures cool, and the days grow shorter again. The leaves turn beautiful colors, and it is harvest time at all the farms. There is little precipitation in the Southwest, so residents can usually count on having a sunny day.

55

Add an adverb to each underlined verb to make the story more vivid.

Pete <u>walked</u> downtown, running a stick down a chain-link fence and listening to the sound it made. As he arrived at the park in the middle of town, he saw Cliff riding his skateboard on the steps by the movie theater.

"Hey," Pete <u>said</u>. "What are you doing here?"

"Um, nothing," Cliff <u>said</u>. "I'm probably <u>going</u> to the movies later with some friends." He <u>paused</u>. "I would have invited you, but you've been busy."

"I know," Pete <u>answered</u>. "I got your note. I'm sorry."

"It's okay," Cliff <u>replied</u>. "Hey, maybe you could come with us."

"Oh no, I can't," Pete <u>said</u>. "I promised Leo and Nate I'd go fishing with them."

"Okay," Cliff <u>said</u>, "I guess that settles who your real friends are."

Pete <u>watched</u> Cliff ride his skateboard down the street and away.

56

Cliff sent the following memo to the eighth-grade class officers. Proofread it for errors.

to Eighth Grade class officers

from, d.j. Cliff

date November 13 20__

Subject, your paying to much for music!

This memo is to inform you that Cliff also known as D.J. Cliff, whom has the best taste in music in the sixth grade has started his own busyness D.J. Cliff's music mania.

I can offer you a special deal for the next dance scheduled for this friday. For only 50¢ per student you can have all of the most popular songs of today instead of amature garbage from a live band.

Contact me today and I will be happy to accomadate all of your needs.

57

The following scene is written using indirect quotations. Change the conversation to direct quotations, and be sure to use quotation marks. Rewrite the scene.

Leo and Nate were walking down the hallway when they bumped into Claire, the eighth-grade's class president. She called to them and asked them to wait. Then she explained that she had received a letter from Cliff.

When the boys read the letter, they were shocked. Leo asked Pete if he had known that Cliff was going to undersell them on the school dance price. Pete answered that he hadn't even known that Cliff was starting a D.J. business.

Pete asked Claire what they were going to do about the dance. Leo wanted to know if their offer to play still stood, or if the class was going to go for the less expensive option. Claire answered that the class officers wanted to hear both acts perform before they made a decision. She said she felt sorry that she might take back her offer to the band, but the class's mission was to make money, and Cliff was offering a good deal.

58

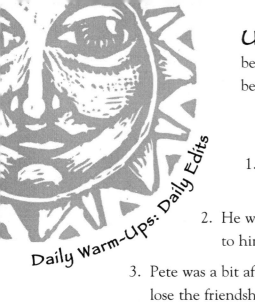

Use coordinating conjunctions from the box

below to connect each group of sentences. Be sure to use a comma before the conjunction. Rewrite the new sentences.

and	but	or	for	nor	yet

1. Pete had never been so angry with Cliff before. He was sorry for Cliff, too.

2. He wanted to talk to Cliff. He wasn't sure Cliff would want to talk to him.

3. Pete was a bit afraid. He and Cliff had been best friends forever. He didn't want to lose the friendship.

4. Would he and his friend be able to work things out? Would this end up destroying their relationship?

5. Finally, Pete screwed up his courage. He called Cliff to talk.

59

Rewrite Pete and Cliff's dialogue using

indirect quotations. Add five adverbs on the lines below to make the story more vivid. Write the revised scene.

"Hey, Cliff," Pete said.

"What do you want?" Cliff asked_____.

"Well, actually, I was calling to find out why you stabbed me in the back," Pete replied_____. "I know you're angry with me, but why did you have to treat me so _____? I didn't mean to hurt your feelings."

"Well, you did hurt my feelings," Cliff said _____, and Pete could hear the sorrow in his voice. "Ever since you joined the band, I've felt that you don't care about me at all."

"That's not true," Pete assured his friend. "I admit I've been distracted, but you're my best friend, and I'll start treating you that way. "So, anyway" he continued _____, "do you want to come watch my practice for the class officers tomorrow?"

"Watch?" Cliff replied. "I'm your competition!"

Use coordinating conjunctions to correct the run-ons in the band review below. Correct the five misspelled words.

This year's Thanksgiving Dance (also known as the Turkey Trot) was a huge sucsess Charlotte Cove Middle School's favorite band, Truck Stop, almost didn't get to play. The band caused some excitement earlier in the week a dispute between band member Pete and his best friend Cliff almost led to the band being canceled. Cliff decided, "If you can't beat them, join them," he decided to collaberate with the band as guest D.J.

D.J. Cliff brought a whole new dimention to the band they still retained the distinctive sound that makes them grate. People seemed to like the mix of classic rock and screeching vinyl, at least they tolerated it. Everyone who attended the dance enjoyed the music one student had a special reason to feel special. Band member Pete debuted his first original song for the band, which was entitled "Chrissie."

61

Circle the word from the pair of words below that correctly completes each sentence. Then write a sentence correctly using each of the words you didn't choose for the sentence provided.

1. Chrissie likes all the vegetables in the cafeteria's new salad bar (beside/besides) the beets.

2. _____

3. (Can/May) I have extra helpings of the beans and rice?

4. _____

5. The students always (compare/contrast) their height by standing back-to-back when they get together.

6. _____

7. That teacher, (who/whom) I know well, used to be a pro wrestler.

8. _____

Daily Warm-Ups: Daily Edits

62

Revise the letter

Samantha wrote her senator to eliminate slang and substitute standard written English. Rewrite the letter.

November 30, 20__

Hey Senator _____,

I'm writing to ask you to introduce legislation to protect the manatees of Florida. I mean, I know they're kinda funny looking, but those animals deserve to be protected from pollution, boat propellers, and loss of habitat just as much as any other species. It really stinks that some people would rather put their own interests above those of an animal who lived in the waters of the Florida Keys long before there were motorboats or real estate booms.

I know you're, like, pretty old school, but I think u should listen to me because I'm a future voter and I could help boot you out of the senate in a few years.

LYLAS (Love Ya Like a Senator),

Samantha

63

Correct the commonly misspelled words in the following passage.

Mr. Klepp looked expecially excited when the students walked into his classroom Monday morning. When the students were seated and quiet, he anounced, "I have some wonderful news. We will be recieving a foriegn exchange student from Scotland."

The students imediately began asking questions: "What is the person's name? Is it a boy or a girl? What's Scotland like? How long will the exchange student stay?"

Mr. Klepp answered, "She is a girl, and her name is Fiona McLeod. She is from a small city called Ayr, which is on the west coast of Scotland, near Glasgow. She is coming in for a few minutes today, but she will be exausted from her journey, and we don't want to embarras her with a lot of questions. I know it's fasinating to learn about someone knew, but we need to understand that it will take time for Fiona to adjust. We mustn't be dissapointed if she's shy and quiet at first."

64

Rewrite the following paragraph in the past tense. For some verbs, you will need to use the past participle.

Fiona's stomach lurches as the car drives up to Charlotte Cove Middle School. She freezes as she steps out of the car into the cold New England air. She reads everything she can about her host state before she comes, but none of it prepares her for how different everything is.

She grows even more nervous as she enters the school and sees her new teacher and classmates. They surround her, smiling and welcoming her. She shakes everyone's hand and becomes more comfortable with every passing minute. She knows she will like her new home.

65

Capitalize the proper adjectives in the following sentence. When you have finished, write three proper adjectives that describe you.

Nobody could understand Fiona! Her scottish accent was so strong that it didn't sound anything like american English. Even worse, she used words that the american kids had never heard of. For instance, she explained, "I'm originally glaswegian," but the kids had no idea what "glaswegian" meant. Was it like being left-handed? It turned out to mean that Fiona had been born in Glasgow.

Sammy explained to Fiona that now she could consider herself a new england girl, or a yankee, if she preferred. Fiona said she wouldn't mind being a "new scotland" girl but that she wasn't fond of being called english, even if it was "new english."

1. _____

2. _____

3. _____

Fiona noticed that Americans frequently use euphemisms for words they consider to be improper or unpleasant. For instance, Americans use the word "bathroom" to mean "toilet," which is the word commonly used in Scotland. Write the more direct word for these common euphemisms. Then think of five other euphemisms of your own and write them.

1. passed away:

2. downsized:

3. sanitation worker:

4. casualty:

5. under the weather:

67

Punctuate the following paragraphs, and correct the five misspellings.

Fiona was embarassed again. She had asked to go to the loo, and it took Mr. Klepp five minutes to get the other students to stop making fun of her. In fact they didn't mean any harm. They thought her accent was adorible however it hurt her feelings when the other students drew attention to her. Consequently she decided to stop speaking entierly.

Meanwhile the rest of the class thought everything Fiona said and did was wonderful for instance all the boys gathered around her at lunch and tried to talk to her. They wanted to make her comftable instead they made her misurable.

Otherwise things were going pretty well for Fiona. She had become very friendly with Samantha and Isabel.

68

Daily Warm-Ups: Daily Edits

Fiona wrote this e-mail home to her parents. Proofread it and correct the errors.

Hello Mum and Dad,

   I'm having a good time at Charlotte Cove, but I wish I could of brought you with me. I like my school I am in Mr. Klepps class he is nice. I have two good friends hear named Sammy and Izzie (Samantha and Isabel are there proper names.) I would of sent you a picture of them, but I cant get my digital camera to work on my host familys computer. By the way Claire and the rest of the Field's say hello. They are super nice, and I'm so glad Ill be living with them for the next six monthes. Claire is all ready a sister to me.

Hear are all the things I miss about home my television shows, my friends, british chocolate (the candy bars here are aweful!), and most of all, you.

Love and kisses,

Fiona

69

Correct the three-way telephone conversation between Fiona, Izzie, and Sammy. Look for incorrect use of reflexive pronouns and homonyms.

Fiona: I keep making a fool of me. Nobody kens what I'm saying.

Izzie: I'm sorry for asking, Fiona, but what does *ken* mean?

Fiona: Och, sea what I mean? It means "know," and its an old Scots word. Yourselves are kind about asking me, but other kids just grown and say, "Their goes Fiona again."

Sammy: Listen, Fiona. Izzie and myself were taking about your problem, and we have an idea. Why don't you teach us some Scottish words, and we'll all use them. Then, when the other kids make fun of yourself, we'll tell them there stupid for not knowing what the words mean.

Fiona: That would be brilliant! Cheers!

Izzie: Um, okay, maybe we'd better start with *brilliant* and *cheers*.

70

The word *strange* is used repeatedly in the dialogue below. Replace it with more vivid and precise synonyms. Then trade with a partner to see if you chose the same words.

Pete: Sammy and Izzie are acting <u>very strange</u>. Suddenly they are using <u>quite strange</u> vocabulary.

Cliff: That's not <u>very strange</u>. They always act <u>pretty strange</u>. What are they up to now?

Pete: They are being <u>really strange</u>. They keep using <u>very strange</u> words that I've never heard of, and then they act <u>strange</u> when I don't know what they're talking about.

Cliff: Huh, that is <u>strange</u>. Any idea where these words might come from?

Pete: Let's put it this way. The <u>strange</u> girl from Scotland seems to know these words, too.

71

Circle the correct verb to go with the subject.

1. All of my friends (is/are) going to the movie.

2. All of the chocolate cake from my birthday party (is/are) gone.

3. Everybody in my class (is/are) able to explain photosynthesis.

4. None of the states in the union (begin/begins) with a B.

5. Corned beef and cabbage (is/are) the traditional meal to eat on St. Patrick's Day.

6. Everyone in my family (is/are) afraid of snakes.

7. (Were/Was) there any holes in your jeans after you washed them in bleach?

8. How many of the players on your team (does/do) your coach think will make varsity?

9. Neither Izzie nor Sammy (has/have) been to Scotland.

10. A bag of softballs (is/are) sitting out on the field.

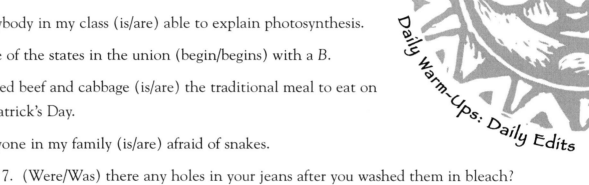

72

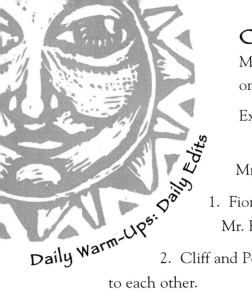

Combine each pair of sentences into one sentence.

Make one sentence a relative clause, and add it to the other to form one sentence.

Example: Mrs. Klepp is a triathlete. She teaches eighth grade at CCMS.

Mrs. Klepp, who teaches eighth grade at CCMS, is a triathlete.

1. Fiona McLeod is from Ayr, Scotland. She is an exchange student in Mr. Klepp's class.

2. Cliff and Pete have been best friends since kindergarten. They live next door to each other.

3. Claire Fields is the eighth-grade class president. She is Fiona's host sister.

4. Mr. and Mrs. Klepp are interested in traveling to Scotland. They met in Australia when they were college students.

5. Mr. and Mrs. Klepp are interested in heirloom sheep breeds. Their students think that's pretty weird.

73

Make sure each underlined pronoun is in the correct number and case. If it is, write C above it. If not, cross it out and correct it.

Mr. Klepp wasn't too impressed with the work <u>their</u> students were doing lately. He wanted to talk to his colleagues about it, so <u>him</u> and Mr. Abdul, <u>who</u> teaches seventh grade, took a run after work to chat. Mr. Klepp explained to his friend, "My students and <u>myself</u> got off to a great start this year, but now <u>they</u> all seem to be slumping, and I can't seem to inspire <u>them</u>. Between you and <u>I</u>, I'm beginning to get worried."

"Hmmm, this is serious," Mr. Abdul said. "Everyone knows <u>your</u> an inspiring teacher, so if you hit a rut, then what must regular guys like <u>I</u> be going through? Are even your best students, like Samantha and Pete, struggling?"

"<u>Them</u> and their friends are all struggling. The other day, Sammy and Isabel had an oral report due. Sammy said that <u>her</u> and Isabel needed an extension because they were having a bad day! I couldn't believe it."

"Sounds like you need to reward the students <u>whom</u> excel and punish those <u>who</u> don't," Mr. Abdul advised.

74

Rewrite the following paragraph so that it has sentence variety.

Mr. Klepp brainstormed ideas to motivate his students. He thought of bribing them with candy. He didn't believe in loading students up with sugar. He thought of offering them a big pizza party. They didn't seem as motivated by food as they used to be. The cafeteria food was much better. They had been supplying it with the food from their class garden. He thought of offering them a class trip to someplace interesting. They had already taken so many field trips. Finally, he decided to make a great personal sacrifice. If the class would raise their average by five points, Mr. Klepp would get a Mohawk haircut.

75

Change the dialogue between Mr. and Mrs. Klepp so that they say the opposite of what is underlined.

Mr. Klepp: Darling, I have decided that, if my students improve their averages by five points, I will get a Mohawk.

Mrs. Klepp: Well, darling, I think that's a <u>mature</u> and <u>sane</u> decision. What made you decide to do it?

Mr. Klepp: I noticed a big <u>balance</u> in my students' averages over the year. During the fall, their grades were excellent. But lately, they have taken a dip. It seemed <u>rational</u> that the grades should go down for no reason, so I decided to fix it with a <u>logical</u> solution.

Mrs. Klepp: Frankly, dear, I think those haircuts should be <u>legal</u> for anyone over thirty. But if your students' grades improve, which is <u>probable</u>, I will take you to the barber myself.

76

Proofread Mr. Klepp's letter to his class.

January 3, 20___

Dear Class,

Someday, I hope to get letters from collige, saying that you are exelling at English, Math, History, and Science, as well as The Arts. I want to see your knowlige of all these subjects grow. I want to help you develop the disipline to make those dreams come true.

When I became a teacher, I pleged to myself that I would become the best Language Arts and Science teacher I could be. I would do anything in my power to get the most milage out of my students that I could. Lately I have been noticeing that my students haven't been doing their best in all of their subjects. In every class, from basic science 101 to advanced biology 103, my students' grades are falling. This is unacceptible to me, and it should be to you.

I am asking you to do your best. Complete your homework every night. If you raise the class average by five points at the end of this quarter, I will get a Mohawk.

Sincerly,

Mr. Klepp

77

Revise the following sentences to make them gender-neutral. Mark your corrections on the sentences.

1. Everybody in the class finished his homework last night.

2. As each of the students left the room, Mr. Klepp reminded him that tomorrow was Career Day.

3. Three students in the class want to be mailmen.

4. Not surprisingly, Izzie wants to be chairman of the board of a huge corporation and be the boss of everyone in her company.

5. Cliff, on the other hand, wants to be a philosopher and inspire all of mankind.

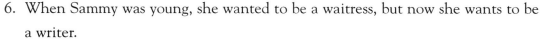

6. When Sammy was young, she wanted to be a waitress, but now she wants to be a writer.

7. A person should not expect to achieve his career goals overnight.

8. Someone who wants to be great should cultivate greatness throughout his life.

9. Many children want to be firemen and policemen when they grow up.

10. Students who enjoy writing and public speaking might want to be anchormen.

78

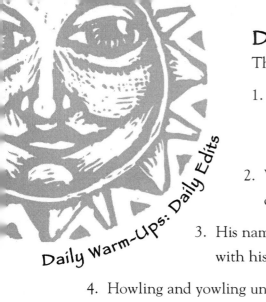

Draw a cartoon that tells the story the way it's written. Then rewrite the story to make clear what the writer meant to say.

1. Mrs. Lamberth watched from her window disgusted as the short, gray-haired man dragged on a leash the dog who had a moustache.

2. With his tail between his legs and his ears laid back, the man had clearly mistreated his dog for years.

3. His name was Mr. Greco and, snarling at a cat, he walked down the street with his dog, Muggsy.

4. Howling and yowling until her owner came, Mrs. Lamberth picked up the cat and lectured Mr. Greco about his cruelty to animals.

5. Calling the Society for the Prevention of Cruelty to Animals, the cat curled around Mrs. Lamberth's feet and purred.

79

Proofread Pete's journal entry for errors.

January 15, 20__

Dear Mr. Klepp,

Tomorrow, as you know, is Bring Your Child to Work Day, and I have a big problem. You see, my father is unemployed. I don't want to embarras myself or him by anouncing that to the class, espeshally because they're are so many kids who's parents have great jobs.

Its not fair that some people don't have jobs. Who's fault is it that my dad's company went out of business? Your probably thinking that my dad's a deadbeat, but theirs no truth to that. He's a great dad and a great worker. He just had bad luck, and now he is exausted with worry about finding a job. He used to do fasinating work—he was a writer of humorus greeting cards—and its hard to find another job like that.

I guess theirs know way around it. I'll hang out with him and see if I can at least cheer him up.

Pete

80

Pete is at home with his dad, who is looking for a job. Help Pete's dad revise a letter of application. Eliminate fragments and run-ons.

January 10, 20__

Dear Sir or Madam:

Enclosed please find my resume and references in application for the position of writer advertised on your website, as you will see from my resume I have been a writer for a long time and I have a lot of experience. Including writing greeting cards. And writing liner notes for CD jackets.

The company for which I was working recently went out of business, it is challenging to find the perfect job in this business climate but I think that I'm a good match for your company. I like writing, and I am a good writer. Looking forward to hearing from you.

Yours truly,

Peter Wilcox, Sr.

81

Proofread Isabel's journal entry to Mr. Klepp.

Dear Mr. Klepp,

Bring Your Child to Work Day was a disastir for me. As you know, I was exited about going to my mom's office, because she is a partner at a law firm, and I'm very proud of her. I wanted her to be proud of me, too. But when I got there, after she introduced me to her colleagues and employes, she stuck me in a room all by myself and asked me to attatch mailing labels and licking envilopes all day. She almost forgot to let me out at lunchtime!

I didn't learn anything about being a loyer, and it was the least glamerus day of my life. I thought I would feel special, but I just felt like one of her lackeys. At the end of the day, when I complaned to her about it, she said, "You learned the most valuble lesson of all. You have to work hard to make it to the top of your proffession, unless you want to lick envelopes for the rest of your life." I still think she just used me.

Your disapointed student,

Izzie

82

Change the following conversation between Pete and Mr. Klepp from indirect to direct dialogue. Be sure to switch paragraphs with each speaker. Rewrite the revised dialogue.

Mr. Klepp took Pete aside after class the next day and asked how he had liked working with his dad. Pete reminded him that his dad was unemployed. Mr. Klepp asked Pete to tell him what he and his dad did, and Pete explained that they had spent the morning writing letters and sending out resumes. Then they went to lunch with a former colleague of his dad's who was working at a company that might need a writer soon. Pete said that his dad had taken him to a job interview in the afternoon. Pete and his dad had both worn suits, and Pete had to wait in the reception area. Mr. Klepp told Pete that looking for a job sounded like a full-time job to him, and he said that Pete's dad seemed to be good at it. Pete agreed and said that he felt very proud of his dad.

83

Correct the verb tenses in the following story, and correct the five misspelled words.

Sammy had been waiting for middle school basketball season for her hole life. She had chose to be a basketball player back in kindergarten, when her mother had brung home the recreation center broshure and asked her if she'd like to join a team. Since then, Sammy had went to every game and every practice she could, and she had spended hours on the court, practicing her jump shots and fowl shots.

Now she had a chance to be on a reel school team. She looked around at her freinds and thought, "I have went a long time waiting for this moment, and I'm not going to forget it." When Izzie passes the ball to her, she sunk the basket and smiled.

84

Correct the verbs in the following story.

Pete and Chrissie had went to the movies together back in November. Pete's mom, Marjorie, had drove to Chrissie's house and picked her up, and they had took the highway to the big multiplex in Richland.

Their first date had went okay. Pete had sweat quite a bit, so his hand had feeled a bit sticky when Chrissie had reached over and grabbed it during a scary part. And she did think it was weird that he had brung homemade popcorn because his mom didn't like him to eat movie popcorn with unnatural ingredients. But they had grew comfortable with each other by the end of the movie, and on the way home, Pete, Marjorie, and Chrissie had set in the car together laughing like old friends.

85

Rewrite the story below in the past tense.

Sammy is running down the court, dribbling the basketball. She looks for an open girl to pass the ball to, but nobody is available. She fakes out the girl who is guarding her, and she drives to the basket. She fakes a shot, dribbles, and shoots a layup that goes into the basket with a swish. She hears the cheers of her friends and family in the stands.

Her coach calls time-out, and she trots over to the bench. Mrs. Klepp, her coach, pats her on her sweaty back and says, "Keep it up, Sammy. You're doing great."

Daily Warm-Ups: Daily Edits

86

Correct the verbs in parentheses to make them the proper tense.

Pete had been wanting to do something special for Chrissie for a long time. They (date) for two months, and she (give) him a really nice birthday present. He (want) to do something nice for her, but he didn't have a lot of money. So he (make) her a present in home economics.

His teacher, Ms. Monroe, (be) surprised at first when Pete had told her that he wanted to make a sundress as his final project. She (think) that he was kidding. But when Pete (explain) that it was a present for his girlfriend, Mrs. Monroe's face (break) into a huge smile, and she (offer) to help Pete choose a nice pattern and a pretty fabric.

87

Correct the sentences below.

1. Izzie likes to play basketball, but she is a real slow runner.

2. Sammy, on the other hand, runs good but dribbles bad.

3. Fiona has never played basketball, so she looks strangely playing the game.

4. She's a natural athlete, though, so she's improving real fast.

5. The team feels well about their chances for victory this season.

6. They have been practicing pretty consistent, and they have been working hardly.

7. They want to win real bad, so they will do anything it takes.

8. Their coach, Mrs. Klepp, plays really good, too.

9. She was a starting forward on her college team, and she was real talented.

10. Now, when she coaches the team, she shouts fierce but she is fairly.

88

Cliff wrote the following article on the basketball game. Eliminate the clichés, and find a novel way to express the ideas.

Girls Blast Rivals in First Basketball Game of Season

This Saturday, the Charlotte Cove Lady Hawks dominated their competition in a 50 to 35 point win over the Richland Raiders.

Our own sixth-grade wonder, Samantha, <u>ran like the wind</u> during several breakaways and scored big for the team, earning 11 points. She was <u>as high as a kite</u> after the game, saying to this reporter, "This is a <u>dream come true</u> for me. I have been <u>waiting my whole life</u> to play this kind of basketball."

Sammy had lots of help from teammate and best friend Izzie, who plays point guard. Izzie has been gaining speed in practice, and now she is <u>as sly as a fox</u> on the court. Izzie said, "<u>There's no 'I' in 'team</u>.' I'm just grateful to be part of such a wonderful group of girls."

89

Valentine's Day is coming, and the students are writing poems for people they know. Revise the similes and metaphors they have written to make them more original.

1. You are as sweet as candy.

   You are as _____ as _____. (for a friend)

   You are as _____ as _____. (for an enemy)

2. You are as lovely as a rose.

   You are as _____ as a _____. (for a boyfriend/girlfriend)

   Your are as _____ as a _____. (for a grandparent)

3. You are my honey.

   You are my _____. (for a teacher)

   You are my _____. (for a sibling)

90

Here is a poem that Chrissie wrote for Pete. Underline all of her similes once and metaphors twice. Then, write a poem for someone you care about, using at least five similes and metaphors.

Ode to Pete

Skinny as an alley cat,

But fierce as a tiger,

Sings like an angel,

His guitar spits fire.

Pete is my hero,

He's brave and true.

He's an umbrella in a rainstorm,

Chicken soup for the flu.

91

Mr. Klepp's students have to use hyperbole, or deliberately exaggerated language, to write tall tales. Rewrite the story below using hyperbole to make it into a tall tale. Trade with a partner, and underline all of the exaggerated language he or she used.

Pete and Cliff were out fishing one day when it began to rain pretty hard. They were getting wet. Cliff wanted to go home, but Pete told him that fish like to bite in the rain. So the boys pulled on their raincoats, put worms on their hooks, and waited for a bite.

Just a minute later, Cliff felt a tug on his line. He began to reel in his line, and Pete got out his net. The boys caught a good-sized fish.

Read this composition by Isabel. Underline all the examples of hyperbole. If the hyperbole is also a simile or a metaphor, underline it twice.

Super Sammy

My friend Sammy is the best basketball player ever to live. She scores about a million points every game she plays, and she towers over all the other girls like a mountain over an anthill.

Sammy has been playing basketball for her whole life. Her mom even called her the "Little Dribbler" before she was born because she could feel Sammy bouncing a basketball in her womb.

Sammy has eyes in the back of her head. She can see what her opponent is going to do even before she decides to do it, and she flies down the court like Superwoman.

93

Another device writers use to create humor is understatement. Read the passage below, and underline the examples of understatement. Then substitute hyperbole for the understatement.

Mr. and Mrs. Klepp were chaperoning the school dance, and Mr. Klepp was trying not to wince as Mrs. Klepp stepped on his feet with her size 10 pointy-toed shoes. Pete had never noticed it before, but Mrs. Klepp was a hair taller than Mr. Klepp. She was five foot eleven in her stocking feet, and Mr. Klepp was only five foot eight. But when Mrs. Klepp wore her high heels, the height difference was a bit more noticeable.

Mr. Klepp loved to dance, but Mrs. Klepp wasn't quite as accomplished a dancer. That didn't stop her from trying to lead, though. She kept trying to maneuver Mr. Klepp as they danced, and he finally said to her, "Darling, I think we should try to avoid dancing into the drum kit from now on. The cymbals aren't supposed to clang quite so much during the slow songs."

"Absolutely, darling," she answered, and dipped him very gently, inadvertently dropping him on his head at the last minute.

Write a paragraph about an embarrassing moment in your life. Use either hyperbole or understatement to add humor to the situation. Trade papers with a partner, and underline each use of hyperbole or understatement.

95

Writers use concrete images to show how their characters are feeling. Underline once the concrete images that show that Mr. Klepp is feeling excited. Underline twice the concrete images that show he is worried. Then write two concrete images that could show that he is scared or angry.

Mr. Klepp had been keeping two secrets. His students could tell something was going on. Mr. Klepp's moustache twitched more. His eyes sparkled more. His dimples dimpled more. But, despite his excitement, he also looked a bit worried. He paced up and down the classroom. He raked his hands through his hair. He jingled his pocket change.

Finally, Izzie said, "For heaven's sake, Mr. Klepp, what are you so excited about?"

"I'm not supposed to talk about that," Mr. Klepp answered mysteriously.

Scared: 1.

2.

Angry: 1.

2.

96

Correct the punctuation in the following story.

Insert the paragraph symbol (¶) to indicate a new paragraph.

Of course as soon as Mr. Klepp admitted he was keeping secrets his students began bothering him relentlessly to tell them. If you tell us we won't even make you get a Mohawk at the end of the quarter if our grades go up Sammy promised. Speak for yourself Cliff said but I do really want to know what's going on. Look Mr. Klepp explained I can't tell you one secret because I promised someone very special that I wouldn't. I can't tell you the other secret because I promised myself that I wouldn't. And I think you have to agree that I'm a special person too. Mr. Klepp smiled smugly.

97

Correct the ten misspelled words in the following passage.

The next day, Mr. Klepp grieted his students at the door with a huge smile of releef. "I can finally tell you my secrets!" he announced when everyone was seeted and quiet. "First of all, your teecher is going to be a published author. I have written a children's book entitled *The Little Tomatoe and His Brother the Potatoe.*"

The class cheared. After the applause, Sammy asked, "What is your other peece of news?"

Mr. Klepp beemed with joy and replied, "Mrs. Klepp and I are going to have a baby to reed my new book to."

Daily Warm-Ups: Daily Edits

98

Here is the text of Mr. Klepp's children's book. Correct the misspellings. Then illustrate the story.

1. The little tomatoe was sad and blew.

2. He said to potatoe, "I don't know what to do!"

3. The bumpey potatoe asked, "What is wrong?"

4. The little tomatoe said, "I don't belong,"

5. "All of my heros are brown and have eyes,"

6. "They're shaped like rockets that fly through the skyes."

7. "I am brite orange and short and squat."

8. Spud said, "You are my heroe, and that means alot."

9. "I think I'm no good," said the modest tomatoe.

10. "If that is your vote, than I'll just have to vetoe,"

11. "You're wonderful, whitty, nobel, and true,"

12. "And if this spud is lyeing, I'll eat my own shoo."

Proofread Samantha and Isabel's invitation.

Correct spelling and punctuation errors.

Your Invited!

To a baby shower for Mr and Mrs Klepp

When Febuary 28 20__ at 230

Where Mr Klepps Classroom

Please bring the following items five dollers for a gift a baked good and a pichur of yourself as a baby (it will be reterned to you after the party.)

100

Combine each of the following pairs of simple sentences using a relative pronoun: who, whom, whose, which, or that. Use each pronoun once.

1. The cake took Sammy and Izzie three hours to bake. It was delicious.

2. The boys photocopied all of the baby pictures to make a collage for the Klepps. The students had brought in the pictures.

3. Mrs. Klepp cried when the students jumped out from behind the door and shouted, "Surprise!" Mrs. Klepp is quite sentimental.

4. Mr. Klepp said the cake was the most delicious he had ever tasted. His father was a pastry chef.

5. The Klepps thanked their students for the party. The Klepps really appreciated them.

101

Correct the common usage errors in these sentences.

1. I read in my history book where Maine used to be part of Massachusetts.

2. Maine became a state in the Missouri Compromise, that was ratified in 1820.

3. Fiona finds it hard to master these kind of American history facts because said facts are not covered in Scottish schools.

4. Her recollection of these facts is improving some as she spends more time in the United States.

5. Of course, she knows much more then her American friends about Scottish history.

6. Most of her friends wouldn't have even heard of William Wallace without they have seen *Braveheart*.

7. American students have a long ways to go before they know the history of the British Monarchy.

8. That there is a subject Fiona's friends will likely never learn.

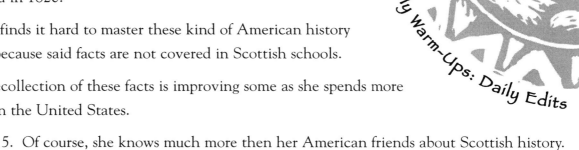

102

Revise the following paragraphs for parallel structure.
Mark your corrections on the paragraphs.

In the springtime, Cliff's thoughts turn to business pursuits. When the grass begins to grow and the weeds coming out, Cliff passes fliers out to all of his neighbors and reminding them of Cliff's Landscaping services. He also has a spring clean-up service and to babysit and pet sitting for people on vacation.

When Cliff cleans out a garage, he does a thorough job of taking out the trash, scrubbing the area, painting and organizes the tools. Homeowners love to see their houses shine and sparkling after Cliff is done. Garden beds also look gorgeous after his pruning and rakes.

Cliff's mom always wonders how a kid with such a messy room can do such a good job of cleaning and organizes other people's stuff.

103

The following story uses the word *mad* repeatedly.
Replace *mad* with a synonym from the box below.

irate	annoyed	angry	upset	bothered
insane	wacky	foolish	absurd	frenzied
crazy	ridiculous	irritated	livid	cross

Fiona was <u>mad</u> at her host sister, Claire, who had invented some <u>mad</u> scheme to get the girls out of going on a family trip. She had told her parents that Fiona couldn't ride in cars for long distances. Claire said it was <u>mad</u> to go on such a long car trip with a girl who might be carsick or throw a <u>mad</u> tantrum in the back seat.

Of course, Fiona was not at all <u>mad</u>, and she felt <u>mad</u> at Claire for giving her host parents such a negative impression of her. To make matters worse, she was <u>mad</u> because she had really wanted to see New York and meet Claire's cousins.

Fiona decided to tell her host parents the truth, even if it made Claire <u>mad</u> at her. After they let Claire know how <u>mad</u> they were at her, the family took off on a <u>mad</u> adventure to New York. Fiona was <u>mad</u> about the city, and she was especially <u>mad</u> about Claire's cousin, Tyrell, who looked even better than in pictures.

Come up with your own synonyms for *nice*, and use them to replace the word in the following e-mail.

28 February, 20__

Dear Mum and Dad,

I'm having a <u>nice</u> time in the United States. Everyone here is being <u>nice</u> to me, and the house where I'm staying is very <u>nice</u>. I think my school is <u>nice</u>, too; my school in Scotland isn't nearly as spacious and well equipped. My teacher, Mr. Klepp, is very <u>nice</u>. He and his wife are expecting a baby soon, which I think is <u>nice</u>.

It's <u>nice</u> to hear from you. I miss you, and I dream all the time of my <u>nice</u> home and <u>nice</u> bed. Please let Granny know that I appreciated the <u>nice</u> sweater she sent me.

Love,

Fiona

105

Read the following pairs of sentences. Write the attitude of the speaker in each sentence: positive, negative, or neutral.

1. Fiona McLeod is a slender young lady. _____

2. Fiona McLeod is a lanky girl. _____

3. Mr. Klepp is an author and educator. _____

4. Mr. Klepp is a schoolteacher who writes children's books.

   _____

5. Samantha is a self-confident scholar. _____

6. Samantha is a conceited smarty-pants. _____

7. Charlotte Cove is a coastal village. _____

8. Charlotte Cove is a rural backwater. _____

9. Pete acquired a previously owned yacht. _____

10. Pete bought a used boat. _____

106

The description below is neutral in its connotations. Rewrite it twice, once as if you were writing a travel brochure to promote it, and once as if you were being critical about the town. Trade papers with a partner, and underline the loaded words in his or her paragraphs.

Charlotte Cove is a village of about 9,000, located on the coast of Maine. The town includes one elementary, one middle, and one high school. Town services provided include fire, rescue, garbage collection, and road maintenance. The town is mostly suburban in character. About fifty percent of the town's residents commute to nearby Richland for work, while the rest of the town's residents work locally in government, small business, fishing, and farming. The town is composed of a downtown area with shops and restaurants, surrounded by suburban neighborhoods and, on the outskirts, rural properties.

107

Use an appositive phrase to combine each pair of sentences. Be sure to set it off with commas.

Example: Fiona is an accomplished fiddler. She is an exchange student at our school.

Fiona, an accomplished fiddler, is an exchange student at our school.

Or: Fiona, an exchange student at our school, is an accomplished fiddler.

1. Nate and Leo are both members of Pete's band. They are in eighth grade.

2. Mr. Klepp is a published author. He teaches language arts at CCMS.

3. Truck Stop is playing at a Battle of the Bands. It is a student band.

4. Sammy and Izzie are starting a band, too. They are two girls in Mr. Klepp's class.

5. Fiona plays the fiddle and sings beautifully. She wants to join the band.

6. Izzie and Sammy are the bandleaders. They're not sure they want someone to join who will only live in town for a few more months.

108

Punctuate the following story.

Fiona was lying on her bed trying not to let her host family hear her crying. She felt completely betrayed and worst of all it was her best American friends who had betrayed her. Because the Battle of the Bands was coming to Charlotte Cove the girls wanted to start a group and try to win the $100 prize but they were also thinking of creating a band that would take the place of Truck Stop when some of the members went on to high school. She had asked them at lunchtime if she could join the band which they had named the Charlottes but they had told her they had to think about it. She had just gotten off Instant Messenger with them and much to her astonishment they had told her that they were going to ask their friend Mei to join the band instead. Fiona had nothing against Mei a talented singer and guitarist in Mr. Abdul's class but she didn't understand why she couldn't be in the band too. What was wrong with her. She was a really good singer and she knew her soprano voice would sound beautiful with Mei's alto. Her fiddle playing which had won her several competitions in Scotland would give the band a unique sound. Totally exasperated she rolled over and tried to get some sleep.

The following paragraph has a number of commonly confused words. Cross out each incorrect word, and replace it with the correct alternative.

The next day of school was a nightmare for Fiona. It's hard when you can't hang around with you're click. During French class, Izzie had scent a note to her, complementing Fiona on her voice and saying she knew they weren't being fare and so fourth, but Fiona couldn't help but recent the way they had treated her. Fiona was confidant that she and the girls would make up, but for now she was happier buy herself. She couldn't altar her feelings, and she was under no allusion that the girls were going to change their minds about inviting her into the band. That decision couldn't help but effect their friendship, at least for a while.

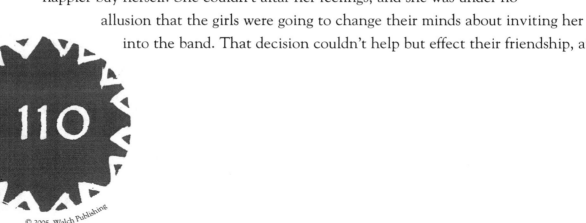

110

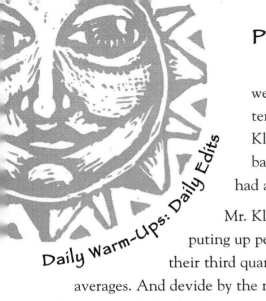

Proofread the following story.

It was the end of the quater, and the students in Mr. Klepp's class were more excited then usual because they had worked harder that term than any other in their lives because they wanted to see Mr. Klepp get a Mohawk. In fact, Cliff had perswaded his dad, who was a barber, to go to school with him, just on the chance that the students had acomplished their goal of rising their class average by five points.

Mr. Klepp desided to turn the report cards into a math game. Without puting up people's names. He writed their second quarter avrages up next to their third quarter scores. He asked students to add up all the second-quarter averages. And devide by the number of students in the class and asked them to do the same with the third quarter column. Finally, he asked them to subtrack the first column from the second column. The result was 5.2. The students howled with exitement. Mr. Klepp was getting a Mohawk.

111

© 2005 Walch Publishing

Use either hyperbole or understatement to describe Cliff's father giving Mr. Klepp a Mohawk. Make your description vivid and funny. Share it with a partner, and notice how your accounts differ.

112

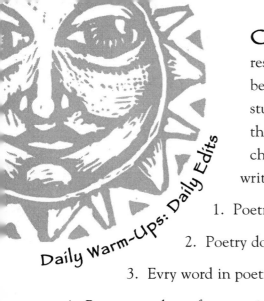

Charlotte Cove Middle School had an artist-in-residence named Ms. Kennedy. She was a poet, and she was going to be working with the students on writing poetry. She asked the students to brainstorm their attitudes about poetry, and this is the list they wrote. Correct the misspelled words on the list. Next, make a check mark next to each of the attitudes with which you agree. Then write three attitudes of your own.

1. Poetry has to ryme.

2. Poetry doesn't have grammer.

3. Evry word in poetry counts.

4. Poetry uses lots of sensery images.

5. Poetry has to use fancey langwage.

6. Poetry is ushally about love.

7. Poetry uses sounds and rythm to create moods.

113

The students in Mr. Klepp's class are writing poems and imagining that they're animals. They are to use all five of their senses. Brainstorm about each animal below. Then, choose one, and write a free verse poem imagining yourself as that animal.

Giraffe:

Grasshopper:

Gorilla:

114

Onomatopoeia is a name for words that sound like what they mean, such as *splat, murmur,* or *buzz.* Underline the onomatopoeia in the following poem, written by Pete. Then, write your own poem using onomatopoeia.

Truck Stop

The clang of the cymbal, the boom of the bass,

The whine of the feedback resounds through the place.

My band is on fire, they riot and roar,

Like race cars and rockets and lions and more.

115

© 2005 Walch Publishing

When writing a paragraph, it is important

to arrange the ideas in some order. Writers commonly use chronological order, spatial order, or order of importance. Outline the topic sentence and main ideas in the following paragraph. Then decide how it is organized.

Pete's neighborhood resembles fishing villages all over the world. The houses in his neighborhood are arranged around the cove, where people have their boats moored. On the shore, there is a boat ramp for putting in and taking out the lobster boats and pleasure boats belonging to those who live in the neighborhood. Alongside the ramp is a dock where skiffs, dories, and tenders are tied. Most of the houses along the waterfront have piles of lobster traps stacked in the front yards, and, in some cases, the boats resting in the side yards are almost as big as the modest houses next to them. Although people think of the front door as the door facing the street, for many the main entrance is the one facing the water and the path down to the docks dotting the shoreline.

116

Write a paragraph describing how to do something simple: tying a shoe, packing your backpack, telling someone you're sorry, or anything you want. Then, trade your paragraph with a partner. Underline your partner's transitions, circle the topic sentence, number the main points, and decide if the paragraph uses chronological order, spatial order, or order of importance.

117

Underline all the transitional phrases in the following paragraph. Tell what order the paragraph is written in.

Pete was going out to dig bloodworms with his Uncle Gus, and he wasn't looking forward to the backbreaking work. First, he had to get up at 4:30 A.M. so that he could put in a full day and get to the flats before anyone else. Next, he had to put on huge hip waders—rubber boots that went all the way up his legs. He wore them right over his pajamas; there was no need to shower when he would be digging in salty muck all day. After he had his legs covered, he put on a thermal undershirt and three sweaters. Outside all of those layers, he wore a raincoat to keep the morning mist off his back. He knew that by midmorning, he would be tearing off the layers, but for now he wanted to be warm. Finally, he ate the big breakfast that his mom cooked for him and waited for Uncle Gus's truck to arrive.

118

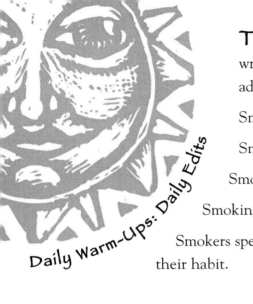

Take the list of information, written in random order, and write a paragraph. Include a topic sentence, use a logical order, and add transitions. Explain why you chose the order you did.

Smoking causes lung cancer, emphysema, heart disease, and stroke.

Smokers' hands and teeth are stained brown.

Smokers have horrible breath; kissing them is like kissing an ashtray.

Smoking is an expensive habit.

Smokers spend lots of time shivering outside public places to indulge their habit.

119

Cliff and Pete want to nominate Mr. Klepp for teacher of the year. They have brainstormed a list of qualities and an example for each. Decide what order they should go in, and write a logical paragraph arguing that Mr. Klepp should get the award.

1. He is creative. He turned an area outside of his classroom into a mini-farm to teach about ecosystems.

2. He is caring. He has helped both Pete and Cliff though hard decisions.

3. He has high standards. He helped students raise their averages by five points.

4. He practices what he teaches. He wrote and published a children's book, and now he's working on a young adult novel.

5. He is fun. He does silly things, such as getting a Mohawk on a dare.

120

Change the following sentences to the past tense. Add capital letters where needed.

1. The ccms lady hawks go to the girls' basketball state championship.

2. The girls are all nervous, but sammy may be the most nervous one on the team.

3. She has led the lady hawks to one of their best seasons ever, and she is only in the sixth grade.

4. She imagines playing on the wnba someday, perhaps for the new york liberty.

5. As she plays, she thinks about the people in the crowd.

6. Maybe there is a scout from a great college team, such as the university of connecticut.

7. Sammy is a little girl with dreams as big as the washington monument.

121

Proofread the following story.

It was the second half of the state championship between the lady hawks and their great rivels the richland raiders. Coach Klepp, who was eight months pregnent, was walking up and down the sidelines nervusly and shouted instructions to her girls. When Izzie made a sloppey pass to Fiona, coach Klepp singled time-out, and the girls' huddeled.

"Izzie, we can't aford that kind of misteak," Mrs. Klepp said.

"I no, coach. I'm sorry." Izzie answered sadley.

"Thats okay, Izzie. Just be sure to look at each other."

"And if your open, speak up, right coach?" Sammy said.

"Absolutely, captain." Mrs. Klepp replied. "Now whose going to win."

"We are." the girls shouted.

Proofread the following story.

All of the mom's and dad's in the audience were wearing Teal and Black, the Team colors for the Hawks'. Some were holding signs that said, "Defence!" and "Fly hi, Hawks!" Sammys parents George and Grace had a sign of their own it said, "Go Lucky 7!" becase that was Sammys' number.

Usually, Grace, Sammys mom, chatted with her friends' when she went to games, but this time she was completly focused on the game. Sammy maid a pass, and Grace shouted, "Good job Chickadee!" Which was her pet name for Sammy. George nudged his' wifes sholder and explaned, "Gracie, star athletes aren't usually called Chickadee."

123

Proofread the following paragraph.

The game was down to the last twenty four seconds, and Fiona had the ball. The score was one hundred and one to one hundred and two, and Fiona knew that the game depended on her. She thought about her options. She could pass the ball to Sammy, but she was double teamed. She could pass the ball to Roxy, but she hadn't been shooting good lately. She could pass it to Izzie the Point Gard but, to be perfectly onest, she was still angry with Izzie. She couldn't forgit that Izzie was the one who had said she couldn't be in the Charlottes, the band that the girls were putting together. She new that shouldn't matter, but . . .

"Fiona I'm open!" Izzie shouted. Fiona looked at the clock. 12 seconds. She chest past to Izzie, who bounced the ball to Sammy, who somehow, miraculusly, faked out her too guards and made a layup for the win! Fiona felt Izzie's and Sammy's arms around her, and she relized she had made the right choise.

124

Write a one-paragraph description of an exciting athletic event you witnessed or participated in. Use at least ten vivid adjectives to describe the experience. Then trade papers with a partner, and underline the adjectives.

125

Proofread the following story.

The girls in the locker room was screaming, laughing, and poured sports drinks on each other. All of them was feeling like winners, and Fiona was no exeption. But she couldn't help but notice that both Izzie and Sammy was getting more attention from the girls and even the coach than her. Everybody were remembering that Izzie had assisted Sammy with the basket, but nobody were remembering that Fiona had assisted Izzie.

Either Sammy or Izzie were calling Fiona's name. She looked over, and Sammy said, "Are you coming?"

"Where." Fiona asked.

"We're haveing a victory party at my house." Sammy answered. "One of us must of told you, right?"

"No," Fiona answered, "Nobody tell me anything. I can't go because my host family and Claire's cousin is taking me to dinner."

"That's to bad," Sammy said, but Fiona wasn't sure she meant it.

126

Read the description of Beau. Underline the sensory images the writer uses to describe him. Which of the five senses does the writer emphasize? Which sense does the writer not use?

Pete and Cliff took Beau, the new kid, to the girls' game. He was the most exotic creature they had ever met. Beau had bright red curly hair, which stood up all over his head like dandelion fluff. He wore little Ben Franklin wire-rimmed glasses, and his braces, which he flashed often in huge smiles, had hot-pink bands. His clothing was odd, too. He wore a grungy pin-striped suit coat that was much too big for him, tight black jeans, a black T-shirt with safety pins stuck in it, and a skinny red tie. The boys were pretty sure he was wearing cologne, too, because he smelled like a combination of sugar cookies and smelly feet. Even during the noise of the game, they could faintly hear punk music blasting from the earbuds of his mp3 player. And when he spoke, it was with a laconic, Cajun drawl as spicy as jambalaya.

127

Using lots of sensory imagery, describe someone you know well. Use as many of the five senses as possible. Then trade descriptions with a partner, and label each of the five senses used.

Daily Warm-Ups: Daily Edits

128

© 2005 Walch Publishing

All the dialogue in the following story is indirect. Turn it into direct dialogue. Remember that Fiona is Scottish and Beau is from Louisiana. Give the reader clues about where they come from. Remember to start a new paragraph for each new speaker. Trade with a partner, check for grammar, and underline examples of regional dialect.

Pete, Cliff, and Beau walked into the local pizza parlor, where they noticed Fiona and Claire at a huge table with Claire's relatives. Pete and Cliff walked to where Fiona and Claire were sitting and introduced them to Beau. Beau told Fiona that he had been very impressed by her pass to Izzy during the last seconds of the game. Fiona thanked him and asked where he was from because she noticed that he had a charming accent.

He told her that he was from New Orleans, said that he thought she had a charming accent, too, and asked what she was doing in Maine. She explained that she was an exchange student. She asked him why he was in Maine, and he explained that his mother had been transferred to a new job.

129

Fiona and Beau were sitting together in the corner of the pizza parlor, amused by all the words New Englanders use. Beau mentioned words like: skidder (a machine to drag wood), dooryard (an old-fashioned word for the area outside one's house) and "dee-yah" (which is what the word "dear" sounds like with a Maine accent). Fiona mentioned that Sammy's mother calls her "Chickadee" (the Maine state bird) and that the girls describe things they approve of as "wicked good."

Brainstorm a list of ten words that are unique to your region or community. Use them in a short dialogue, and read the words you chose in class to see how many others chose the same words.

130

Combine each pair of sentences into a complex sentence using one of the following subordinating conjunctions: *since, because, before, after, although, where, until, while*. Write original sentences using the conjunctions you don't use. Remember that *before, after, since,* and *until* may also be used as prepositions.

1. Orchestra practice was before school at CCMS. Fiona always dreaded it.

2. She was from Scotland. School started much later in the morning.

3. She thought she was going to have a bad day. She saw Beau standing with an electric guitar in the strings section.

4. He obviously loved music. She hadn't expected him to be a "band geek."

5. She screwed up her courage. She stood next to him and plugged her electric fiddle into his amplifier.

131

Combine the following sentences using the
subordinating conjunction or relative pronoun provided. When
you have finished, think of another way you could combine the
sentences.

1. Beau wasn't surprised to see Fiona with a fiddle. He knew that
   Celtic music was popular in the United Kingdom. (because)

2. Fiona didn't know that fiddles were also popular in Cajun music.
   Beau played Cajun music. (which)

3. Beau asked Fiona to play a little bit of a Celtic song he knew before
   practice started. Fiona blushed furiously. (who)

4. She played the song. Tears came to Beau's eyes. (when)

5. Fiona asked Beau to play her something. He played her a bit of a zydeco song. (so)

132

Finish the following sentences in any way you choose.

1. Although it may seem old-fashioned, _____.

2. Until I was six years old, _____.

3. Because Pete is an only child, _____.

4. When I think of summer, _____.

5. Before I travel, _____.

6. So that we surprise our parents, _____.

7. While Cliff wasn't looking, _____.

8. Wherever you go, _____.

9. As if the screaming fans weren't enough, _____.

10. As I walked down the spiral staircase, _____.

133

© 2005 Walch Publishing

Sammy and Izzie are on the telephone. Revise their conversation by replacing the underlined words with more interesting choices.

Sammy: Isn't that new kid an <u>awesome</u> guitar player?

Izzie: Yes, he's <u>great</u>.

Sammy: I was thinking he would make a <u>good</u> addition to our band. What do you think?

Izzie: Well, he is a <u>great</u> guitarist, but the Charlottes is supposed to be a girl band.

Sammy: So, maybe we add one "Charlie." Let's face it; our band is pretty <u>bad</u> right now.

Izzie: That's true. Wouldn't it be <u>bad</u> to invite him, though, when we didn't invite Fiona?

Sammy: But Fiona plays the fiddle, which would sound <u>bad</u> in a rock band.

Izzie: I know. But I think she feels <u>bad</u> that we didn't invite her.

134

Rewrite the following scene, using direct instead of indirect dialogue. Remember to start a new paragraph for each new speaker.

At lunchtime, Samantha and Isabel set down their trays next to Beau. Sammy told him that she had heard him playing during orchestra practice in the morning. She said that she really admired his playing a lot. Izzie explained that she and Sammy both play instruments, too. Sammy plays the drums, and she plays electric bass, although she plays stand-up bass for the school orchestra. Beau said that he had noticed them playing and that they were very good. Sammy asked him if he had considered joining a band outside of school. She told him that she and Izzie had started a band and that they needed a good guitarist. Beau said that was interesting, but that he was already putting together a band with a talented fiddler. Just then, Fiona sat down next to him and smiled sweetly at the girls.

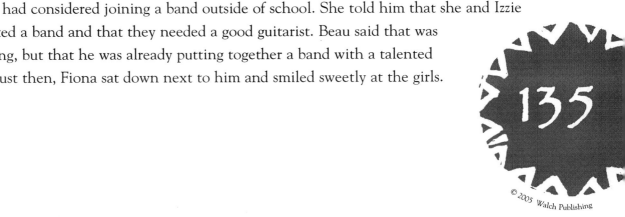

135

Read Pete's description of his favorite place. Underline the sensory images, and write what sense they describe. Correct the ten misspelled words.

To me, Fenway Park is the most beutiful place in the world. Built for the Boston Red Sox in 1912, it is the oldest major league stadeum still in use in the United States. The Red Sox have won many games there, incloding the World Series after an eighty-four year hiatis, in 2004. When I walk into Fenway Park, I smell cut grass, prezels, hot dogs, and sunscreen. Thinking about it now, I can almost taste the delicious mountins of junk food I've eatin there—nachoes dripping with cheese, salty pretzels bigger than both my hands, fizzy sodas that tingle on my tounge. I can see the beautiful pattern cut into the green grass of the dimond, and I can see the streetlights sparkling on top of the wall called the Green Monster in the outfield. Best of all, I can hear the crack of the bat and the roar of faithful fans cheering their beloved Sox.

136

Read Fiona's description of her favorite place. Underline examples of hyperbole, and correct the ten misspelled words.

The Aisle of Skye, also known as the Mistey Island, is my favorite place. The mountans, shrowded in clouds, stretch to infinaty, and the midsummer days go on forever. Each emereld hillside is covered with a million grazeing sheep, and you can drive the durt rodes for days before you meet another traveller. Skye is truly a magical place.

137

Read Beau's description of his favorite place. Underline all his similes and metaphors, and label them. Correct the ten misspelled words.

My favorite place is my Granddaddy's home on the bayou. It has shutered windows like big sleepy eyes and a poarch as wide and comferting as my grandmother's lap. Jasmine and honeysuckle rap the house in a big embrace, and their fragrence floats threw the air like music. Life on the bayou isn't perfect; there are mosquitos as big as my ear and aligators as fierce as a bear defending its cub. It's steamier than a sauna and wilder than any jungle, but to me it's paridise.

138

Read Cliff's description of his favorite place. Underline examples of understatement, and explain why the understatement in the passage tells how enormous the Internet is.

My favorite place isn't a place at all. It's a virtual place called the Internet. It must be pretty puny, because the whole thing can fit onto the fifteen-inch screen of my computer. There's a little picture gallery in it called the Louvre, which has a couple of relatively well-known works of art. The Internet is big enough to hold a pretty good-sized market, too. Billions of items are for sale on online auction sites, which makes for a nice selection.

139

Write a description of your favorite place. Use sensory images, similes and metaphors, and hyperbole. Then trade descriptions with a partner, and underline and label the descriptive techniques.

Daily Warm-Ups: Daily Edits

140

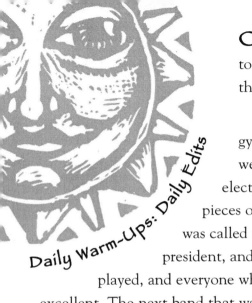

Change the following story from the passive to the active voice, and eliminate unnecessary wordiness. Rewrite the story.

The dress rehearsal for Battle of the Bands was being held in the gymnasium by the CCMS Student Council. One of the things they were checking for was to make absolutely, positively sure that all the electronic equipment—microphones, amps, lights, and other important pieces of electronic equipment—was working. The first band, Truck Stop, was called to the stage by Claire, who was also the eighth-grade class president, and they got ready for their first song to be played. Their song was played, and everyone who was present agreed that the band sounded very excellent. The next band that was up to rehearse was a band that was relatively new called the Charlottes. The thing was that all of the people that were members of the band and played in it were sixth-graders, and so they were not expected by the rest of the kids to be that good. Nothing could be further from the truth; instead, all of the rest of the students who were present thought that the band was really very excellent, also.

141

Insert adjectives and adverbs in the spaces provided. Trade with a partner, and compare your stories.

Sammy, Izzie, Fiona, and Beau's band, the Charlottes, was the most _____ band CCMS had ever seen. The combination of Fiona's _____ fiddle, Beau's _____ guitar, Izzie's _____ stand-up bass, which Beau had encouraged her to use, and Sammy's _____ drums gave the band a sound like _____. The vocals were _____, too. Beau and Fiona harmonized like _____, and the sound of their voices intermixing was _____. When Izzie joined, and they sang in three-part harmony, it was _____. When Mr. Klepp listened to the band, he said, "I have heard _____ music, but I have never heard anything so _____ in my entire life."

142

Revise the following paragraph. Mark your corrections on the paragraph.

The members of Truck Stop was getting worried. They had been the most popular band all year, but now they had a rivul that were just as good as, if not better then, they was. Truck Stop were a good band, but there music was pretty convensional. They did alot of covers of other peoples music, and they mostly play songs that are heard on the radio. The Charlottes were a different kind of band. They played a multicultural mix of zydeco, celtic, afro-carribean, and punk music that nobody had ever heared before.

143

The CCMS Student Council wrote a letter to parents, asking them to chaperone the Battle of the Bands. Revise it to eliminate slang and make it more formal in tone.

March 15, 20__

Yo Moms and Dads,

Remember when you were young? Remember how majorly important your social life was to you? Remember how you didn't want your dorky parents coming to your rock concerts? Well, times have changed, and this little note is to invite you to our Battle of the Bands as a chaperone. I know, you probably think middle school bands are lame. But that's cuz you haven't been to CCMS, home of some of the best student bands in the state. Besides, without you guys, the principal won't let us have our gig. So come, okay? There's a sign-up sheet at the bottom of the page, which you should fill out and stick in your kid's backpack. And tell them that if they don't bring it in, you'll take their bike or something, okay, cuz we really need your help.

Thanks a bunch,

CCMS Student Council

144

The following Battle of the Bands advertising flyer is written in overly formal language. Revise it so that its tone is appropriate for its audience.

We Hereby Request Your Presence at

The Battle of the Bands

To be conducted at the Charlotte Cove Middle School Gymnasium

On Friday the Thirtieth of March

In the Year 20__

Musical Guests include

Truck Stop

The Charlottes

The Bumps

Charlotte Cove Jazz Ensemble

Accolades for Victory Include

A Musical Videotape produced by One-Hit-Wonder Productions

One Hundred Dollars

The Adoration of CCMS Listeners

145

Proofread the following story.

Mr. Klepp was haveing difficulty makeing the students in his class pay attention to his lessons. He kept stateing the same information over and over again, because nobody was paying attention. Instead, everybody was worrying about the upcoming Battle of the Bands. He decideing to bring in copies of his young adult novel to read to the class.

Creating an imaginary world in fiction is a tricky job. Mr. Klepp had used qualitys of his students in his fictionel characters, and he was a bit worryed that his students would feel betraied about appering in his book. Would they think the characters were likeable? He desided that revealling the storys to the students ahead of time was the easyest solution.

146

Mr. Klepp has written descriptions of characters loosely based on his students. Pete wants to revise the description of his character to be more glamorous and manly. Help him replace the underlined words with synonyms that carry more attractive connotations. Write Pete's revised description in the space below.

Pat was a <u>gangly, goofy</u> boy with a <u>shock</u> of black hair <u>that stood straight off his head</u>. His face was <u>peppered with freckles</u>, and his <u>bushy eyebrows</u> gave him a <u>perpetually confused</u> look. At school, Pat <u>loped</u> down the corridor, <u>knocking</u> into kids with his <u>bony elbows and knobby knees</u>. The only time he was graceful was when he <u>cradled his guitar like a baby in his arms</u>.

147

Cliff wasn't pleased by the fictional description of him, either. Help him to choose words that sound more mature. Rewrite Cliff's description in the space below.

Clyde's <u>chubby cheeks dimpled</u> when he smiled, which was all the time. His <u>button nose</u> turned up so much on the end that he looked as if he could drown in a rainstorm. His <u>stringy red hair hung in his eyes like a curtain</u>, which might explain why he was so <u>accident-prone</u>. His <u>baggy jeans, riddled with holes, hung well below his hips, revealing a well-worn pair of boxers</u>.

Daily Warm-Ups: Daily Edits

148

Proofread this description of Fiona's nightmare the night before Battle of the Bands.

The lights came up on Fiona's band, and suddenly she was playing a song she had never heard before, called "Do You Want to be a Failure"? She had expected to play "Punk Rhapsody", a song she and Beau had written together months ago. Why was she playing this new song instead of "Punk Rhapsody?" How was she supposed to know her part, when Beau had just shoved it under her nose and said, "Play this?" It was especialy horrible because when she looked down at the music, Beau's face looked up at her and screamed "Don't dissapoint me"!

Fiona awoke exausted and embarassed. Her dream had been fasinating, and it was somewhat humoros now that she was awake. She imediately rolled over and went back to sleep, hoping that her exitement about tommorow wouldn't cause her any more bad dreams.

149

Create sentence variety in the newspaper article below. Also eliminate run-ons and fragments. Trade papers with a partner, and check each other's work. Then write the revised article.

Battle of the Bands Extravaganza at CCMS

On March 30, CCMS hosted the Battle of the Bands it brought the musical talent of the school together to vie for the coveted position of best band at CCMS winning the competition also carried a couple of prizes having a music video produced by One-Hit-Wonders, a local production company, and $100.

There were two favorites going into the competition. Truck Stop, a band that has played at several school events this year. And the Charlottes, a relatively new band composed of four sixth-graders Beau, Fiona, Samantha, and Isabel.

What happened that night though was a total surprise instead of either of those bands winning a group called The Bumps came out of nowhere to win first prize. Even more surprising. The Bumps was made up entirely of teachers Mr. Klepp, Mrs, Klepp, Mr. Abdul and Ms. Monroe which didn't seem fair because she's the music teacher but the Student Council looked over the rules and there's no rule that says that teachers can't compete.

150

Proofread the following story. Then figure out what all the underlined words have in common, and write your answer in the space below.

Every spring the sixth grade at CCMS took a trip to Camp <u>Kutituk</u> in the wilds of Maine. Their, students learned to canoe and <u>kayak</u>, enjoied listening to the <u>peep</u> of spring frogs, and savored the warm <u>noon</u> sun shinning on there backs.

When the kids arrived at the camp, they're councilors, <u>Ada</u>, <u>Bob</u>, <u>Otto</u>, and a guy knicknamed <u>Radar</u>, were their to greet them. As soon as they had settled into there bunks, the counselors played a <u>gag</u> on them. <u>Radar</u> shouted, "Ready, aim, fire!" and they pulled water balloons out from behind their backs. The kids were at first terrifyed, but they laffed when they realised it was a joke.

151

There are several words that are spelled differently in American English than in British English. Find the words Fiona spells the British way, and change them to American spellings.

10 April, 20__

Dearest Mum and Dad,

   We are at Camp Kutituk now, and I'm having a lovely time. It seems the sky is never grey here, and there's nothing to do all day but practise sports, draw colourful pictures in arts and crafts class, savour the fresh air and sunshine, and enjoy the flavours of bug juice (a kind of fruit punch) and hot dogs.

   At the end of the week here, we are to put on a humourous theatrical programme, and I am to play a princess. I can't wait!

Love and kisses,

Fiona

152

The students wanted Mr. Klepp to play a song at the camp talent show. Here are some lines from a song they wrote. Fill in the other lines, using the same rhythm and rhyme scheme as the first stanza.

1. We're the kids of Charlotte Cove,

2.

3. We kept our campfires burning bright,

4. We played all day and slept all night.

5. The kids at Charlotte Cove are cool,

6.

7. We miss our friends and families, too,

8.

9.

10. But now it's time to leave this place.

153

Revise Pete's letter home to his parents to give it more sentence variety and stronger verbs. Then write the revised letter. Compare your letter with a partner's.

April 20, 20__

Dear Mom and Dad,

   We're leaving tomorrow. I am sad to leave. I am happy to be coming home. Camp was okay. We did some fun stuff. I learned to kayak and make beaded jewelry. We did some games to learn trust. We did survival skills.

   Last night was the talent show. Mr. Klepp won again. I can't believe it. He keeps doing contests for kids. He keeps winning. This time I was in his band. The whole class was. That was better than losing to him again.

   I'll be home soon. See you then.

Love,

Pete

154

Proofread the following story for titles that should be underlined or italicized, placed in quotation marks, or capitalized. Correct the five misspelled words.

On the bus ride home from Camp Kutituk, Mr. Klepp and the class played a trivea game called "Stump the Chump." They had to quiz Mr. Klepp on his knowlege of rock music, books, and films.

"Okay, Mr. Klepp," Pete started. "Who sings I Want to Be a Lifeguard?"

"That's easy," Mr. Klepp answered, "the b-52s. Who sings Stairway to Heaven?"

"led zeppelin, of course," Sammy said. "Even I knew that. What is the name of the movie staring John Travolta and Olivia Newton-John?" she asked.

"Um, I think its called Fat," Fiona said.

Everybody laughed and Sammy explained, "No, it's Grease, silly!"

"I've got one," Mr. Klepp said. "Does anyone know who wrote War and Peace?"

"Is that a song?" Beau asked.

"No, it's one of the great works of russian litrature, written by Leo Tolstoy.

Proofread the following story.

When the class got back from camp, their greenhouse garden was overflowing with fresh vegtables. Mrs. Klepp's class had taken care of LuLu, the classes' goose, but nobody had weaded the gardin. There were tomatos so ripe that they bent their vines. Heads of lettice were crouding each other out, and pea pods were bursting their seems. Carats were poking their orange heads out of the ground, and magenta beats were sweling out of the ground.

"Looks like it's time to harvist!" Mr. Klepp proclamed when they got back to school. The kids spent their sience class out in the greenhouse, diging up the froots of their labers.

Add each phrase where it works best: *both/and, either/or, neither/nor, not only/but also.* Correct the misspelled words.

The next day, ( ) Mr. Klepp ( )Mrs. Klepp was in school. The class speculated about what might be going on. "( ) Mrs. Klepp is having her baby, ( ) they decided to give up teaching and join the circus," Pete gessed.

The kids were dissapointed that Mr. Klepp was gone, but they were exited to have a substatute, because they figured ( ) the substitute ( ) Mr. Klepp would not expect them to get real work done. What a surprise it was when their substitute, Dr. Bodwell, recquired them to memorise ( ) the Periodic Table of the Elements ( ) a Shakespearean sonnet!

157

Proofread Cliff's journal entry to Mr. Klepp.

April 30, 20___

Dear Mr. Klepp,

I'm glad you and Mrs. Klepp are finnaly having the baby, but I've got to tell you it's having a horrible affect on your class. We were alright the first day, but things just keep getting worst. Dr. Bodwell is so strick, he never gives us a brake and we have to do the most boaring stuff you wouldn't believe me if I told you. We spent like three days just doing grammer! We never get any piece and quite from his nagging.

I need your advise Mr. Klepp. I've became much better behaved than I formally was, but having this substitute is making me loose my mind! What can I do to keep my moral up and not end up at the principle's office?

Your desparate student,

Cliff

158

Revise the following birth announcement:

Konrad and Julie Klepp are proud to announce the birth of their daughter Chloe McGraw Klepp. Chloe was born at richland hospital at 959 A.M. on april 30 20___. She wayed 8 lbs and 2 oz Mother and daughter are both helthy and resting comfortable.

Chloe's grandparents are Konrad Klepp Sr and his wife Maria of Richland and Reginald Grover and Louise McGraw of ames Iowa. Chloe also has seven ants and uncels and 12 cusins on her fathers side.

159

Proofread Dr. Bodwell's note to Mr. Klepp.

May 3, 20___

Dear Konrad,

Thank-you for intrusting me with you're students. They were quite well, with a few exeptions. (See attatched list.)

Durring my time in your class room, we studied grammer, cemistry, and do creative writting. I have left foulders of the student's work on your desk.

I hope you have a marvellous time with your new baby. Fatherhood, as I'm shure youll descover, is a wonderfull experiance.

Your's truely,

Bud Bodwell, PhD

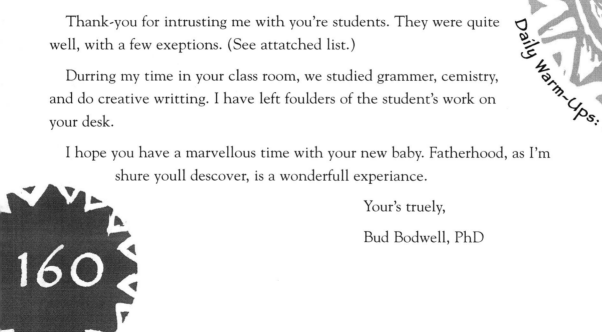

Daily Warm-Ups: Daily Edits

160

Proofread the following passage.

Every May, CCMS held elections for class offisers and for student counsel representatives. There were six posisions for each class: presedent, vise presedent, secretery, and tresurer, plus two student counsel representatives.

Several students in Mr. Klepps class was planning to run. Either Sammy or Izzie were going to run for president, and the other won would run for vise president. Cliff, whom had lots of experiance working with mony, was runing for tresurer, and Pete was planing to run for student counsel representative.

161

Proofread Principal Perez's speech.

Welcome Perspective Class Offisers and Representitives;

Congradulations on your dicision to run for elective office at CCMS. Particapation in student-run goverment is both a dutey and a privelage. Students elected by their piers have a great deel of responsability. They must speek not only for themself, but also for there fello students.

Don't be feerful about that burdan, but don't take it to litely, either. Run a desent campane, treat your oponents with respect, and your classmates will respect you. Good luck to all.

162

Correct the errors in the following campaign slogans.

Each candidate has three. Vote for your favorite slogan for each student, and explain why you prefer it. Or, write a better slogan, if you prefer.

1. Sammy and Izzie: An Adminastration for the Enviorment!

2. Cleen up ccms, vote for Sammy and Izzie as Presidant and VP

3. Do things Different: Vote for Sammy and Izzie

4. A vote for Cliff is votes for Cash

5. Cliff is Real Funny, He'll Take Care of You're Money

6. Cliff: Responsable, Sensable, and Wize

7. Vote for Pete he's a good lissener.

8. Pete Rock's! Elect him for you're Representitive

9. Vote Pete for student Counsel he'll make youre prefrances known!

163

© 2005 Walch Publishing

Revise Cliff's speech to add more variety to his sentence length and structure. Correct the five misspelled words.

My Fellow Sixth-Graders:

I would like to be your treasurer. I am a hard worker. I am good with money. I am trustworthey. I get good grades.

I do have good friends in this class. I won't play favrites as treasurer. I will listen to everybody. I will collaberate with Principal Perez and the teachers.

I will come up with good fundrasers. I will keep careful track of our classes money. I will make sure we have the cash for a good trip in the eighth grade.

Thank you for your vote.

Revise Samantha and Isabel's speech.

Classmates, Teachers, Staff, and Principle Perez:

Our names are Samantha and Isabel and we are running for co-presidents of the sixth-grade class, we believe that we can make a big difference in the enviorment of this school.

Every day people through out hundreds of pages of paper. Valuble soda cans and plastic bottles. Not to mention the waist that the kitchen produses.

Our class is all ready doing alot to kombat environmentel problems, we have a greenhouse that we razed money for, and we do composting and recicaling in our class, but we want to take it to a school-wide level.

165

Revise Pete's speech to eliminate clichés and correct the five misspelled words. Rewrite the speech.

Friends, Teachers and Ms. Perez:

Being your representative to the Student Council would be a dream come true for me. I believe that children are the future, and I want to be a leader for the future. I know that good comunication is key, and I will do my level best to be a sholder to cry on and a rock to len on.

I know that actions speak louder than words, so here is a list of my acomplishmennts in the sixth grade: I am a band member, an honor student, and a member of the soccer and baseball teams.

I believe a friend in need is a friend indeed. I am asking for your vote as your friend, and I promise to be your friend in student goverment.

Proofread the following passage.

The time for campaning had finally came to an end, and the students were voteing. To celabrate the ocassion, Mr. Klepp was waring an Uncle Sam outfit, with a red, and white stripped hat and a fake beerd.

All of the kids had fighted hard for their positions, and they had knew from the begining that some of them would half to loose. Still they wished they could of all won.

That afternoon, Ms. Perez the principal red the names of the winners over the intercom. Amazingly, all of the kids from Mr. Klepp's class who had ran were winners.

167

Think about policies or problems at your school that you'd like to change. Write a short speech to your school community in which you outline the problems and what you would do to solve them. Trade with a partner, and offer suggestions for revision.

168

Proofread the following for capitalization, spelling, and punctuation.

The first job of the CCMS student council was to plan events for the end of the year. They had to prepare for the following events, eighth-grade graduation, step-up day for incoming sixth-graders, a final assembly, and field day.

Claire who only had a few weeks left as president before she moved up to High School was in charge of events. She put students on commitees Pete was on the field day team, Cliff was in the step-up day groop, Isabel was on the graduation committee, and Sammy was on the assembly committee.

169

Pete is designing a Field Day schedule. Proofread his timetable.

Feild Day Agendah

730–830 A.M. flag football sixth grade versas 7th grade
eith grade vs teachers

830–930 A.M. winner of sixth seventh grade verse winner of
8th grade v teacher's

930–ten A.M. three legged race

10–11 pie eaten contest

11–12 outdoor consert

Isabel was in charge of writing an invitation for family and friends of eighth-graders to attend the Eighth-Grade Graduation. Revise her invitation to make it sound more formal. Correct the five misspellings.

To Eighth Grader's Folks

Come On Down to the Eighth-Grade Gratuation ceramony

From about 12:00–1:30 P.M.

Friday, June 5, 20___

Too people can come for every graduet.

Proofread Fiona's e-mail to her parents.

1 June, 20__

Dear Mum and Dad,

I can't beleive that I will be home in two weeks? Living in the US has bin fun nonetheless I want to get home to the farmiliar places and people I love so much. I know you want me to try and pack lightly however I have got so many wonderful preasents and suvenirs here that I don't no if I will be able to cut down no more than I all ready have.

I'm sending some photoes of the people in my class so that youll finely be able to put names with faces. Beau my boyfriend is the one with the wild ginger hare.

Love and kisses,

Fiona

172

Beau wrote an e-mail to his best friend in Louisiana. It is unnecessarily formal and verbose. Revise it to make it sound more friendly and informal.

June 1, 20___

My Dear Reginald,

Springtime in New England is divine: the trees, after a seemingly endless hiatus, have renewed their greenery, and flowers have blanketed the verdant hillsides. The air is warm and pleasant, and a gentle sea breeze plays across my coastal town.

Love, I am pleased to report, has bloomed with the flowers of springtime. My longtime infatuation with Fiona McLeod has, at long last, matured into a romance. I enclose a portrait of her, so that you can admire her beauty as much as I do.

With fond memories,

Beau

173

Mr. Klepp asked his students to write about their plans for summer vacation. Revise Cliff's response.

This summer I plan to ride in an airplain for the first time in my hole life! I am going to Florida to see my Grandmother and Grandfather. I love grammie and gramp, and I haven't seen either of they since they moved to the south last year. We use to be next door naybors, so I have mist them a real lot. My faverite Uncle who's name is jimmy is comeing with me, so I wont be aloun.

174

Here is Fiona's description of her plans for the summer. Proofread for errors and eliminate hyperbole.

As you know I'm going back to Bonnie Scotland in to short weeks time. I feel like I have been in maine forever nothing against this beautiful place but I really want to get back to my family and friends.

I have had the most stellar time imaginable with you and this class. You are the best people on the planet, and when I return to Scotland, I will tell everybody I see how wonderful you've been to me.

175

Proofread Pete's description of his plans for the summer.

I burn real bad when I go out in the son, so I'm going to stay in my room and practise my gitar for, like, hours. I whant to come back to school next year as the leader of the new Truck Stop, cuz if I don't take over, the bands going to be in reel trouble. I'm hopeing that Izzie, Sammy, and Beau will join with Chrissie and I to form a new group, because were both two small without one another.

I'm also exited about going to ball games with my dad, fishing (with lots of sunscreen on of coarse) and ridding my bike to Cliff's house.

176

Proofread Sammy's plans for the summer.

As you can imagine I have a bussy summer planned for myself this year, I'm going to three camps bowdoin college music camp, hoops basketball camp, and overnight camp at camp kutituk. I also want to work on some plans I have for the recycling program at school I'm thinking about working with the town too so that we can collect waist from area busnesses and houseolds too. Of course, I will also spend plenty of time hangeing out on the beach so don't worry about me!

177

Fiona and Beau have to say goodbye to each other, because Fiona is going back to Scotland. Change their indirect dialogue to direct dialogue. Then rewrite the dialogue.

Fiona and Beau were standing in the lobby of the airport with Beau's mom and Fiona's host family. Fiona hugged her host parents and sister first, and she thanked them and told them that she would never, ever forget them. She gave an extra hug to Claire and told her that she had always wanted a sister, and now she felt she really had one. Claire told her that she felt the same way, and that she was going to come visit Scotland as soon as she could. Then Fiona turned to Beau. They were both crying. The rest of the group moved away so they could be alone for a minute. Beau hugged Fiona and told her that he had never loved anybody before, and he wasn't sure he could love anybody ever again. Fiona said she felt the same way. Beau promised her that he would write every day. Fiona said that she would, too, and she promised to send him lots of pictures on e-mail. Beau said that he would get a job and save up money to visit her. Finally, it was time to part. They hugged each other for the last time, and Fiona walked away.

Combine Mr. Klepp's simple sentences to give them more variety. Then rewrite his letter.

June 10, 20___

My Dear Students:

Thank you for a wonderful year. I have treasured each one of you. Pete, I hope to see you in concert one day. Cliff, I expect to see your landscaping truck driving down the streets of Charlotte Cove in the near future. Your green thumb has been priceless in our garden. Sammy, I expect to see you run for president someday. I will vote for you. I know I will be seeing Izzie this summer. She has already started babysitting for Chloe. She's a wonderful babysitter. Beau, I'm so glad you joined our class this summer. I will see you at the beach. I know you plan to take the junior lifeguard course. Fiona, thank you for gracing our school with your gentle presence this year. I won't forget you.

Mrs. Klepp and I will be doing what we always do this summer. We will travel a bit. We will enjoy the harvest of our garden. We will savor the short but precious Maine summer. This summer will be different, though. We will have a baby girl to share it with. I will be a diaper-changing machine. I can't wait.

179

Now describe your plans for the summer. Then share your writing with a friend.

180

To save space, paragraph breaks have not been maintained in this Answer Key.

1. *September, Dear, Middle, School, I'm, Tuesday,* and *Sincerely* should be capitalized. *Class, exciting,* and *yourself* should be lowercase. *Dear, Welcome, exciting, together,* and *Sincerely* are misspelled. **2.** In paragraph one, *weird, field, scruffy, moustache,* and *buttoned* are spelled incorrectly. *Smiles* should be *smiled.* The final sentence of paragraph one is a fragment. In paragraph two, *their* should be *there* in the first sentence, and *to* should be *too.* In the second sentence of paragraph two, *They're* should be *There,* and *piece* should be *peace. John Lennon* should be capitalized. *Hippie* is spelled incorrectly. In paragraph three, *begins* should be changed to *began.* **3.** Answers will vary. **4.** Sentences will vary. Misspelled words are *freedom, classes, strict, assign,* and *a lot.* **5.** In paragraph one, *you* should be capitalized. *No* should be *not. Wate* should be *wait.* There should be a comma after *minute* and an *I* after *but. Real* should be changed to *really.* In paragraph two, *I been* should be changed to *I have been.* There should be a *but* after *grow up* or a period after *up* and followed by *Right.* In paragraph three, there are two run-on sentences, which can be corrected in a variety of ways. *Rite* should

be *write,* and *ryme* should be *rhyme. Good* should be changed to *well. Ill* should be *I'll.* **6.** The story should be punctuated as follows: "Hey, are you Pete?" Leo asked, tapping him on the shoulder. ¶ Pete turned around defensively. "Yeah," he said, "what do you want?" Pete was feeling paranoid about the older kids after stories he'd heard of practical jokes. ¶ Leo answered, "I'm your big buddy. Mr. Klepp asked me to show you around school because we're both musicians." ¶ "Really? What do you play? Are you in a band? What grade are you in?" Pete had suddenly lost his shyness. ¶ "Um, let me see if I can remember all your questions," Leo replied. "I'm in eighth grade. I play drums in a band called Truck Stop, and we play everything—rock, pop, punk, reggae, you name it. And we're looking for a guitarist who can write songs." ¶ At that, Pete was speechless. **7.** Answers will vary. **8.** In the heading, there should be colons after *TO, FROM, DATE* and *SUBJECT. Parents, students, Cove, School, Principal, September, Dress,* and *Code* should all be capitalized. There should be a comma between 15 and 20__. In the first paragraph of the body, *dress code* and *middle school* should be lowercase. In the second sentence, there should be a colon after *school.* In the third paragraph, there should be a colon after *address. Dress*

Code Committee, Charlotte Cove Middle School, Charlotte Cove, Maine should all be capitalized. There should be a comma between Cove and Maine. **9.** Passage should read: "Quiet down, please," Mr. Klepp asked, but it was no use. Students were reading the memo from Principal Perez in disbelief. "Look," Mr. Klepp said, "rather than complaining pointlessly, let's have a discussion about the memo." ¶ Cliff immediately moaned, "No ripped clothes? There goes my whole wardrobe." He threw the memo down in disgust. "What skater has clothes that aren't ripped?" he asked. ¶ "Skaters who don't fall off their boards all the time, Cliff," Mr. Klepp answered. ¶ "I can understand most of the rules," Samantha said, "but why no flip-flops? Are my toes offensive to the administration?" ¶ "Maybe you should ask them," Mr. Klepp replied. "For homework, please draft a letter in response to Principal Perez's memo." **10.** Answers will vary. **11.** In paragraph one, sentence one, *was* should be *were* and *through* should be *throw*. In sentence two, *isn't* should be *wasn't* and *shure* should be *sure*. In the third sentence, *was* should be *were*, *probley* should be spelled *probably*, and *teem* should be spelled *team*. In paragraph

two, sentence one, *sees* should be *saw*. In sentence two, *was* should be *were*, and *fourth* should be spelled *forth*. In the third paragraph, *calls* should be *called*. In the fourth paragraph, *say* should be *said*. In the fifth paragraph, *laughs* should be *laughed*. In paragraph six, *asks* should be *asked*. **12.** Cliches are *easy as pie; couch potato; show her the ropes; fish out of water; you can't teach an old dog new tricks; if at first you don't succeed, try, try again; second wind; let's get this show on the road.* Revisions will vary. **13.** Misspelled words: *Slitely* should be *Slightly*, *Story's* should be *Stories*, *Novel's* should be *Novels*, *Wiches* should be *Witches*, and *Alices* should be *Alice's*. List of short stories should read as follows: "Harrison Bergeron" by Kurt Vonnegut, Jr.; "The Gift of the Magi" by O. Henry; "The Lottery" by Shirley Jackson; "Thank You, Ma'am" by Langston Hughes. List of novels should read as follows: The Chocolate War by Robert Cormier; The Witches by Roald Dahl; The Outsiders by S. E. Hinton; Alice's Adventures in Wonderland by Lewis Carroll. **14.** Incorrect verbs: *red* should be *read*, *cryed* should be *cried*, *studyed* should be *studied*, *wrote* should be *written*, *heared* should be *heard*, *replyed* should be *replied*, *set* should be *sit*, *learning* should be *teaching*, *sat* should be *set*, and *begun* should be *began*. **15.** Answers will vary. **16.** Poster should read: Attention All Students: Please come to the Fifth Annual Halloween Social! Who: All your friends in the sixth, seventh, and eighth grades What: An evening of games, ice cream, and local bands Where: The gymnasium When: This Friday Why: To have fun and raise money for the eighth-grade class **17.** In paragraph one, *reconize* should be spelled *recognize* and *six* should be changed to *sixth*. In paragraph two, *Froot Loops* should be capitalized, and there should be commas after *Loops* and *school*. *Theirs* should be changed to *There's*, *Jazz Ensemble* should be capitalized, and there should be a comma after *Ensemble*. There should be a comma after *band*, and *Truck Stop* should be capitalized. In paragraph three, *your* should be *you're*, *Im* should be *I'm* and *Truck Stop* should be capitalized (two times). In paragraph four, *seventhe* should be *seventh*. In paragraph five, *forgotten* should be *forgot* and *real* should be *really*. In paragraph six, *wrighting* should be *writing*, *Friday* should be capitalized, and *wate* should be *wait*. **18.** Answers will vary. **19.** *Sit* should be *Set*, and *perimiter* should be spelled *perimeter*. *Lie* should be *lay*, and

clothe should be *cloth*. *Three hundred* should be *300*. *Lites* should be spelled *lights*. *Pore* should be spelled *Pour*, and *bole* should be spelled *bowl*. *Carve* should be capitalized, *pumpkins* should be lowercase, and *deccorations* should be spelled *decorations*. *Bye* should be spelled *Buy*, and *Halloween* should be capitalized. *Get* should be capitalized. *Sit* should be *Set*, and *bored* should be *board*. *Dores* should be *doors*, and *lets* should be *let*. **20.** Answers will vary. **21.** Answers will vary. Some possibilities: 1. Isabel was angry because Cliff wrote all over her planner. 2. Before she went to Mr. Klepp to tell, she decided to ask Cliff why he had done it. 3. Cliff saw the look on Isabel's face, and he got worried. 4. He didn't think writing on her planner was a big deal, but, obviously, she did. 5. He decided to apologize, since she was so upset. 6. Isabel saw how sorry he was, so she felt better. 7. She told Cliff she wouldn't tell Mr. Klepp if he promised not to do it again. 8. After they shook hands, Isabel went to recess. 9. Cliff was putting on his coat when he saw Sammy's planner. 10. Although he knew he shouldn't, he got out his markers and wrote on Sammy's planner. **22.** Sentence punctuation will vary. Misspelled words are as follows: In paragraph one, *are* should be *our*. In paragraph two, *assinements* should be *assignments*, *doo* should be *due*, and *privet* should be *private*. In paragraph three, *handel* should be *handle*. In the postscript, *becase* should be *because* and *looser* should be *loser*. **23.** Passage should read: Cliff showed Pete the note in the hallway. "Can you believe this?" he asked. "They're such babies. I say we get our revenge." Pete wasn't sure. He relied on his planner, too. In fact, he was kind of a neat freak, and he had to admit that Cliff was a disorganized slob. Pete also thought it was mean for Cliff to be messing with the girls' stuff, but he didn't want Cliff to think he was a geek. Pete said, "I don't know, Cliff. Is it really worth getting detention to bother scribbling on a couple of planners?" "Oh, I'm way past planners now," Cliff answered. "This is all-out war." **24.** Answers will vary. **25.** The story should read as follows: Mr. Klepp was sitting at his kitchen table and grading his students' quizzes. He noticed that Pete had brought his grade up from a C to an A–. He corrected Kyle's test and noticed that he was still having a hard time keeping dates straight. When he got to Isabel's paper, he smiled. He knew how much knowledge she had on the

subject, how much she loved ancient cultures, and how many books she had read on the subject. As he started to grade the paper, he noticed something weird. Some of Isabel's answers were in a different handwriting. The ones in her writing were correct, but the ones in the black scribble were wrong. He knew she knew the right answers, but he did not know what had happened. Next he got to Sammy's paper. It had the same black scribbles and the same incorrect answers. He recognized that writing, but he didn't know whose it was, until he got to Cliff's paper. Mr. Klepp was going to need to discipline someone tomorrow, but it wasn't the girls. **26.** The following words are misspelled: In paragraph one, *ment* should be *meant*, *knowlege* should be *knowledge*, *hole* should be *whole*, *expectently* should be *expectantly*, *suttle* should be *subtle*, and *triumphent* should be *triumphant*. In paragraph two, *validety* should be *validity*, *towerd* should be *toward*, *ansers* should be *answers*, *mached* should be *matched*, *apperes* should be *appears*, *cheeting* should be *cheating*, *condem* should be *condemn*, and *shore* should be *sure*. In paragraph three, *colum* should be *column*, *confidantly* should be *confidently*, *offen* should be *often*, *nieghbor's* should be

Daily Warm-Ups: Daily Edits

neighbor's, and dismised should be dismissed. **27.** Answers will vary. **28.** Answers will vary. Here is one possibility: Mr. Klepp, it's true. I did change the answers on Sammy's and Izzie's papers, but I did it for a good reason. They're snobs, and they think they are so smart. I wrote some notes in their planners because I was trying to be friendly. They wrote me a letter and said I was a loser. They said I don't do my work and am disorganized. They said they'd do stuff to me if I did anything again. Maybe trying to be their friend wasn't a good idea, but I was trying to be nice. I'll never do that again. I got caught because I'm not as sneaky as they are, but they're just as bad. **29.** Dialogue should read: Isabel: If you wanted to be our friend, why didn't you just talk to us? Cliff: I thought you would think I was stupid. You're both so smart. Isabel: Writing on our planners didn't exactly make you look like a genius. Samantha: Besides, we don't think you're stupid. We think you're cool. Cliff: You always make fun of me when I say the wrong answer. Isabel: Sometimes we feel unpopular, so we make fun of the popular kids because being smart is all we've got. Sammy: Hey, we've got each other! Cliff: Well, maybe we can hang out when I get

back. Sammy and Isabel: Where are you going? Cliff: Mr. Klepp suspended me for a day. I'm going to the retirement home to volunteer in the cafeteria. **30.** Answers will vary. Here's one possibility: Cliff climbed the old, rickety steps to the old folks' home. As he opened the front door, he thought he could hear voices whispering about him. With shaking knees and a quivering voice, he walked up to the front desk and said, "I'm Cliff, checking in for work." When Cliff was five, his grandfather had gone into a retirement home. Cliff felt frightened to meet the patients when he remembered his grandfather lying in a bathrobe and smoking a cigar. The head nurse, Mr. Blythe, smiled at Cliff and reassured him that he would just be serving the residents soup. **31.** 1. Bernice was a woman who had helped to build aircraft carriers and raised a family during World War II. 2. A man called Grant had flown a crop duster all over the Midwest when he was in his twenties. 3. Louis remembered migrating from Oklahoma to the West during the Dust Bowl. 4. Minnie was a vaudeville star who had performed in a dance number at the Grand Ole Opery. 5. A couple named Mr. and Mrs. Suzuki, who were Japanese-American, had been placed in an internment camp by the U.S. government during World War II. **32.** Samantha: What was life like during the Great Depression? Mr. Wilson: We were very poor, Sammy. All of the people I knew were poor. At first my mother, father, and I traveled around the country looking for work, but then my dad got a job building bridges for President Roosevelt's WPA project, a government program to give us Depression-era families some relief. Samantha: Did you have a job? Mr. Wilson: All of us worked. My brothers and I did chores around the house and worked in the garden. My mother raised us kids, kept the house, and cooked all the food for my brothers and me. **33.** Isabel: Where did you grow up, Grammie? Grammie: We lived on the Lower East Side of Manhattan, in New York City. Isabel: Describe your apartment. Grammie: We lived in a tenement house. We had to climb four flights of stairs to get to our place, and there was no hot water. Everybody hung laundry out the windows, so walking down my alley was like being under a circus tent. My grandparents, who had emigrated from Russia, lived in the apartment below us, and my mother's sister and her family lived next door. My life was filled

with family. Isabel: What did your father do? Grammie: He worked on the railroad as a Pullman porter. My mother worked for the Bell Telephone Company as one of the first operators. **34.** Pete: What did you do for work during the 'thirties? Gramp: I was a guitar player in a Hawaiian band. Pete: Are you *kidding*? That's so cool! Gramp: Yes, we were pretty cool. My band and I traveled all around New England in our Model T Ford. We gave concerts, offered lessons, and even did radio advertisements. Pete: Wait, I thought you said you lived in Hawaii. Gramp: No, we just played Hawaiian-style music. It was popular around the country then. **35.** Pete and Cliff were in the cafeteria. Pete had brought lunch from home, but Cliff had bought a school lunch. They were comparing their meals. "Hey Pete, how's the liverwurst?" Cliff asked, looking over at Pete's mushy bread and smelly cold cuts. "It's the worst lunch my mom makes," Pete complained. "She knows I hate it, but she thinks the protein will make me the most intelligent kid at school. How's your lunch?" Pete asked. "It's the most disgusting food I've ever eaten. The peas are the mushiest and the chicken is the most fatty I've ever had. The

Daily Warm-Ups: Daily Edits

pudding is the lumpiest on the planet." "Look at how many kids waste their food here," Pete said. "We should start a petition to get better food." "Yeah," Cliff agreed, "and we should ask for someone who can cook well, too." **36.** Cliff and Pete walked into Mr. Klepp's classroom to complain about their lunches. They noticed that he was eating a beautiful green and purple salad with bright red tomatoes, yellow peppers, and crusty croutons in it. He also had some lovely hard-boiled eggs in the salad. "Hey, where did you get that?" Pete asked. "I made it," Mr. Klepp answered. "What do you mean?" Cliff asked. "Did you go to the salad bar at the store and put it together?" "No," Mr. Klepp answered, "I made it. I grew the vegetables in my garden, and I raised the chickens that laid the eggs in my backyard." "Oh," the boys said. "That sounds like a lot of work." "Not if you love it," Mr. Klepp replied. "Would you boys like to see my garden?" "Field trip to Mr. Klepp's house!" the boys shouted, as the rest of the class came in from lunch. **37.** Answers will vary. Here is one possibility: The children felt excited as their bus driver took them up the dirt road to Mr. Klepp's house. Actually, it seemed more like a farm than a house. One

difference about Mr. Klepp's house was that it had one side that had been made from glass. "That is my greenhouse, class," Mr. Klepp told the class. "I start vegetables out there early in the spring, and I can even have tropical fruit in the long, cold Maine winters when I keep my fruit trees in there." Another difference about the house was that instead of a backyard with grass, Mr. Klepp had planted vegetables. He took the students back to the garden, and each of the students picked fresh vegetables for a huge salad, which Mr. Klepp served to them at lunch. **38.** As Mr. Klepp's students munched on their salad and a crusty loaf of bread that Mr. Klepp had baked that weekend, Sammy saw something out the window that made her jump. "Mr. Klepp!" she screamed, "There is a giant white chicken running around in your backyard!" "That's not a chicken," Mr. Klepp laughed between bites of salad. "That's a goose. Her eggs are in the quiche you're eating right now." "I'm going to be sick," Isabel said. In the meantime, Sammy was out of her chair and running to the backyard to meet this adorable goose. Mr. Klepp called, "Wait!" but it was too late. No sooner had Sammy started chasing the goose than the goose turned around, honking like a lunatic, and started chasing Sammy! **39.** "Thanks for taking us to your farm, I mean house," Cliff said when they got back to class. "I think that was the best food I've ever eaten." "Me, too," Sammy added. "It was cool to see where food comes from. I'd never pulled a carrot from the ground before, or picked lettuce." "Hey," Pete said. "If you can have a farm in your yard, why can't we have one at school?" "Okay," Isabel said. "We could give the vegetables and eggs to the cafeteria, and maybe our school lunch would taste better." "Well," Mr. Klepp said, "I do teach biology in the sixth grade." He thought for a moment. "Yes, I think it's a great idea!" he said. "But it will cost money to get the supplies. We'll have to do some fund-raising." **40.** Answers will vary. **41.** The topic sentence is *Being in a band isn't easy, because for every minute on stage, you have to spend an hour doing other stuff.* The following misspelled words should be corrected: *minuet* should be *minute*, *reherses* should be *rehearses*, *instraments* should be *instruments*, *blisturs* should be *blisters*, and *grate* should be *great*. The sentence that does not belong is *I have a dog named Chico that howls every time I play "Stairway to Heaven."* **42.** Topic sentences

will vary. In paragraph one, *bred* should be *bread*, *lie* should be *lay*, *spred* should be *spread*, *Forth* should be *Fourth*, and *faceing* should be *facing*. In paragraph two, *clowds* should be *clouds*, *feirce* should be *fierce*, *leafs* should be *leaves*, *hided* should be *hid*, and *unpluging* should be *unplugging*. **43.** The topic sentence is *Mr. Klepp's classroom is unlike most sixth-grade classrooms.* The following misspelled words should be corrected: *ecosystums* should be *ecosystems*, *composte* should be *compost*, *effectivly* should be *effectively*, *principle* should be *principal*, and *theyd* should be *they'd*. The sentence that does not belong is *I went to school years ago in a small town in Ohio.* **44.** Answers will vary. **45.** Answers will vary. Misspelled words: *frusterated* should be *frustrated*, *cords* should be *chords*, *regreted* should be *regretted*, *dieing* should be *dying*, and *triing* should be *trying*. **46.** "I wonder what's wrong with Pete," Nate said. "I don't know," Leo answered, "but I'll find out." He laid his drumsticks down and headed for Pete's tree house, which Leo knew was his favorite place to go when he was feeling upset. As he rode his bike up to Pete's house, he saw Marjorie, Pete's mom, mowing the front lawn. "Have you seen Pete? He left practice without saying goodbye,"

Daily Warm-Ups: Daily Edits

Leo explained. "I didn't notice him come in, Leo," she said. "I've had the lawn mower going full blast, and I must not have heard him." "I'll check in the tree house," Leo said, but Marjorie had started the lawn mower again and couldn't hear him. **47.** all right, course, hear, you're, lead, It's, loser, then, waste, plain. **48.** *altogether* should be *all together*, *already* should be *all ready*, *brake* should be *break*, *dessert* should be *desert*, *shown* should be *shone*, *piece* should be *peace*, *quite* should be *quiet*, *you're* should be *your*, *threw* should be *through*, and *wreak* should be *reek*. **49.** As the other students left for lunch, Pete stayed behind to talk to Mr. Klepp, who was erasing the board. Pete cleared his throat, hoping to get Mr. Klepp's attention. "Um, Mr. Klepp, are you busy?" Pete asked. "No, of course not," Mr. Klepp answered. "What's on your mind?" "Well, I was wondering if you've ever liked a girl." Pete stopped and blushed furiously. "I mean, I'm sure you've liked a girl, but the thing is, I like a girl and I don't know what to do about it." "You have come to the right place," Mr. Klepp said. "I was known in my teenage years as Konrad Klepp, most desperate kid at Morse High." "What did you do about it?" Pete asked, although he was

afraid to hear the answer. "I did what any self-respecting guitarist would do," Mr. Klepp answered. "I wrote her a song." "Wow, that's brilliant!" Pete said. On the way to recess, he grabbed his notebook and a pen. **50.** Answers will vary. **51.** Answers may vary. Here is one possibility: Pete arrived at school ten minutes early. He had arranged to meet Mr. Klepp to play him his song about Chrissie; he didn't want anybody else to hear him. When he arrived at the classroom, Mr. Klepp was at his desk eating a huge bowl of something weird. "What is that stuff?" Pete asked. "It's granola, yogurt, and fruit," Mr. Klepp answered. "Do you want to try it?" "Uh, no thanks," Pete answered. "I brought you my song; do you want to hear it?" "Does a dog yelp when someone steps on its foot?" Mr. Klepp replied, somewhat strangely as usual. Pete ignored the question. "Okay, here goes," Pete began. He cleared his throat, got out his guitar and sang, "Oooooh Chrissie/ you're so pretty/ you got lips like rubies/ and skin like a baby." Pete looked up and asked, "Is that good so far?" "Excellent," Mr. Klepp answered; his eyes were twinkling mischievously though, and Pete wondered if he really liked it. **52.** Letter should read: November 15, 20__ Dear

Truck Stop members, The eighth-grade class is planning a dance to be held on the Friday before Thanksgiving break, and we were wondering if you would play. We know it's short notice, but you were the favorite band at the social earlier this year, and we would really like to have you as our band. The class would be willing to pay you twenty percent of the money we earn. We are going to sell tickets for five dollars, so you would earn a dollar for everyone who comes to the dance. You would need to play between 7:00 and 10:00 P.M., and you would need to set up and strike your equipment that evening. Please let us know if you are willing to play. Thank you for considering our offer. Sincerely, Claire Fields Eighth-Grade Class President **53.** Answers may vary somewhat. Here is one possibility: When Pete got to band practice, he saw his friends gathered around a letter. They had their heads together, and they were talking quietly. For a minute, Pete thought they were talking about him. Chrissie looked up and saw Pete. She said, "Oh my gosh, Pete. Look at this!" She ran over to him, holding the letter and jumping up and down. She handed him the letter, and when he was finished reading she gave him a

big hug. "Isn't it great?" she asked. "Yeah, it's great," Pete replied, tucking the lyrics of his new song in his back pocket and thinking that he'd like to surprise her with his new song at the dance. **54.** Hey Pete, I have come to see you every day this week, and you haven't been here. I have been calling you every night, but I guess you didn't get your messages because you never called me back. I don't know if you are angry with me. If you are, you don't have any good reason. I haven't done anything to you. All of your friends are beginning to think you don't like them. They are saying, "Pete is too good to hang out with sixth-graders, now that he is in a band." If you don't want them to think that, then you should pay attention to your real friends, like me. Signed, Cliff **55.** The two paragraphs should be divided as follows: ¶The Northeast has four distinct seasons: winter, spring, summer, and autumn. During the New England winter, temperatures drop, and there is often snow. Rivers and lakes turn to ice, but the ocean is too large and too salty to freeze. The days are short, and the nights are long. During the northeastern spring, the days lengthen, buds appear on the trees, and the whole world seems to come to life. Summers in the

Northeast are warm and dry. Summer is the main growing season of the Northeast. In autumn, temperatures cool, and the days grow shorter again. The leaves turn beautiful colors, and it is harvest time at all the farms. ¶Some people prefer to live in a climate that is more consistent. For them, the Southwest is an ideal setting. Although there are definitely seasonal changes in the Southwest, temperatures are dependably warm during the day and cool at night. There is little precipitation in the Southwest, so residents can usually count on having a sunny day. **56.** Answers will vary. **57.** Memo should read as follows: TO: Eighth-Grade Class Officers

FROM: D.J. Cliff

DATE: November 13, 20___

SUBJECT: You're paying too much for music!

This memo is to inform you that Cliff, also known as D.J. Cliff, who has the best taste in music in the sixth grade, has started his own business: D.J. Cliff's Music Mania. I can offer you a special deal for the next dance, scheduled for this Friday. For only 50¢ per student, you can have all of the most popular songs of today, instead of amateur garbage from a live band. Contact me today, and I will be happy to accommodate all of your needs. **58.** Answers will vary. **59.** Answers may vary. Here's one possibility: 1. Pete had never been so angry with Cliff before, yet he was sorry for Cliff, too. 2. He wanted to talk to Cliff, but he wasn't sure Cliff would want to talk to him. 3. Pete was a bit afraid, for he and Cliff had been best friends forever and he didn't want to lose the friendship. 4. Would he and his friend be able to work things out, or would this end up destroying their relationship? 5. Finally, Pete screwed up his courage, and he called Cliff to talk. **60.** Answers will vary. **61.** Conjunctions will vary. *Sucsess* should be *success, excitment* should be *excitement, collaberate* should be *collaborate, dimention* should be *dimension,* and *grate* should be *great.* **62.** 1. besides 3. may 5. compare 7. whom. Sentences will vary. **63.** Answers will vary, but students should change *Hey* to *Dear* and change the , to a : They should substitute more formal language for *I mean, kinda funny looking,* and *really stinks.* They should change *u* to *you.* They should eliminate the unnecessary *like* and change *old school, boot you out,* and *LYLAS.* **64.** *Expecially* should be *especially, anounced* should be *announced, recieving* should be *receiving, foriegn* should be *foreign*, *imediately* should be *immediately*, *exausted* should be *exhausted*, *embarras* should be *embarrass*, *fasinating* should be *fascinating*, *knew* should be *new*, and *dissapointed* should be *disappointed*. **65.** Change verbs to *lurched, drove, froze, stepped, had read, could, came, had prepared, was, grew, entered, saw, surrounded, shook, became, knew, would like.* **66.** Scottish, American, American, Glaswegian, New England, Yankee, New Scotland, English, New English. The three proper adjectives will vary. **67.** Passed away: died; downsized: fired; sanitation worker: garbage collector; casualty: person killed or injured in war; under the weather: ill. **68.** Fiona was embarrassed again. She had asked to go to the loo, and it took Mr. Klepp five minutes to get the other students to stop making fun of her. In fact, they didn't mean any harm. They thought her accent was adorable; however, it hurt her feelings when the other students drew attention to her. Consequently, she decided to stop speaking entirely. Meanwhile, the rest of the class thought everything Fiona said and did was wonderful; for instance, all the boys gathered around her at lunch and tried to talk to her. They wanted to make her

comfortable; instead, they made her miserable. Otherwise, things were going pretty well for Fiona. She had become very friendly with Samantha and Isabel. **69.** Hello Mum and Dad, I'm having a good time at Charlotte Cove, but I wish I could have brought you with me. I like my school; I am in Mr. Klepp's class, and he is nice. I have two good friends here named Sammy and Izzie. (Samantha and Isabel are their proper names.) I would have sent you a picture of them, but I can't get my digital camera to work on my host family's computer. By the way, Claire and the rest of the Fields say hello. They are super nice, and I'm so glad I'll be living with them for the next six months. Claire is already a sister to me. Here are all the things I miss about home: my television shows, my friends, British chocolate (the candy bars here are awful!), and most of all, you. Love and kisses, Fiona **70.** Fiona: I keep making a fool of myself. Nobody kens what I'm saying. Izzie: I'm sorry for asking, Fiona, but what does *ken* mean? Fiona: Och, see what I mean? It means "know," and it's an old Scots word. You are kind about asking me, but other kids just groan and say, "There goes Fiona again." Sammy: Listen, Fiona. Izzie and I were talking about your problem, and we have an idea. Why don't you teach us some Scottish words, and we'll all use them. Then, when the other kids make fun of you, we'll tell them they're stupid for not knowing what the words mean. Fiona: That would be brilliant! Cheers! Izzie: Um, okay, maybe we'd better start with *brilliant* and *cheers*. **71.** Answers will vary. **72.** 1. are 2. is 3. is 4. begins 5. is 6. is 7. Were 8. does 9. has 10. is **73.** 1. Fiona McLeod, who is from Ayr, Scotland, is an exchange student in Mr. Klepp's class. OR Fiona McLeod, who is an exchange student in Mr. Klepp's class, is from Ayr, Scotland. 2. Cliff and Pete, who live next door to each other, have been best friends since kindergarten. OR Cliff and Pete, who have been best friends since kindergarten, live next door to each other. 3. Claire Fields, who is Fiona's host sister, is the eighth-grade class president. OR Claire Fields, who is the eighth-grade class president, is Fiona's host sister. 4. Mr. and Mrs. Klepp, who met in Australia when they were college students, are interested in traveling to Scotland. OR Mr. and Mrs. Klepp, who are interested in traveling to Scotland, met in Australia when they were college students. 5. Mr. and Mrs. Klepp are interested in heirloom sheep breeds, which their students think is pretty weird. **74.** *their* should be *his*, *him* should be *he*, *who* is correct, *myself* should be *I*, *they* is correct, *them* is correct, *I* should be *me*, *your* should be *you're*, *I* should be *me*, *Them* should be *They*, *her* should be *she*, *whom* should be *who*, *who* is correct. **75.** Answers will vary. **76.** immature, insane, imbalance, irrational, illogical, illegal, improbable **77.** In paragraph one: *collige* should be *college*; *exelling* should be *excelling*; *Math, History, Science* and *The Arts* should all be lowercase. *Knowlige* should be *knowledge*, and *disipline* should be *discipline*. In paragraph two: *pleged* should be *pledged*, *Language Arts* and *Science* should be lowercase, *milage* should be *mileage*, *noticeing* should be *noticing*, *Basic Science 101* and *Advanced Biology 103* should be uppercase, and *unaccptible* should be *unacceptable*. In the closing, *sincerly* should be *sincerely*. **78.** Answers will vary. **79.** Answers will vary. Here are some possibilities: 1. Disgusted, Mrs. Lamberth watched from her window as the short, gray-haired man with the moustache dragged the dog on a leash. 2. The man had clearly mistreated his dog, who had his tail between his legs and his ears laid back, for years. 3. His name was Mr. Greco, and he

Daily Warm-Ups: Daily Edits

walked down the street with his dog, Muggsy, who snarled at a cat. 4. The cat howled and yowled until Mrs. Lamberth picked it up and lectured Mr. Greco about his cruelty to animals. 5. As Mrs. Lamberth called the Society for the Prevention of Cruelty to Animals, the cat curled around her feet and purred. **80.** In paragraph one: *embarras* should be *embarrass*, *anouncing* should be *announcing*, *espeshally* should be *especially*, *they're* should be *there*, *who's* should be *whose*. In paragraph two: *Its* should be *It's*, *Who's* should be *Whose*, *Your* should be *You're*, *theirs* should be *there's*, *exausted* should be *exhausted*, *fasinating* should be *fascinating*, *humorus* should be *humorous*, and *its* should be *it's*. In paragraph three: *theirs* should be *there's* and *know* should be *no*. **81.** Answers will vary. **82.** In paragraph one: *disastir* should be *disaster*, *exited* should be *excited*, *employes* should be *employees*, *attatch* should be *attach*, *licking* should be *lick,* and *Envelopes* should be *envelopes*. In paragraph two: *loyer* should be *lawyer*, *glamerus* should be *glamourous*, *complaned* should be *complained*, *valuble* should be *valuable*, *proffession* should be *profession*. In the closing, *disapointed* should be *disappointed*. **83.** Answers will vary. **84.** Sammy

had been waiting for middle school basketball season for her whole life. She had chosen to be a basketball player back in kindergarten, when her mother had brought home the recreation center brochure and asked her if she'd like to join a team. Since then, Sammy had gone to every game and every practice she could, and she had spent hours on the court, practicing her jump shots and foul shots. Now she had a chance to be on a real school team. She looked around at her friends and thought, "I have gone a long time waiting for this moment, and I'm not going to forget it." When Izzie passed the ball to her, she sank the basket and smiled. **85.** Pete and Chrissie had gone to the movies together back in November. Pete's mom, Marjorie, had driven to Chrissie's house and picked her up, and they had taken the highway to the big multiplex in Richland. Their first date had gone okay. Pete had sweat quite a bit, so his hand had felt a bit sticky when Chrissie had reached over and grabbed it during a scary part. And she did think it was weird that he had brought homemade popcorn because his mom didn't like him to eat movie popcorn with unnatural ingredients. But they had grown comfortable with each other by the end of the movie, and on the way home, Pete, Marjorie, and Chrissie had sat in the car together laughing like old friends. **86.** Sammy was running down the court, dribbling the basketball. She looked for an open girl to pass the ball to, but nobody was available. She faked out the girl who was guarding her, and she drove to the basket. She faked a shot, dribbled, and shot a layup that went into the basket with a swish. She heard the cheers of her friends and family in the stands. Her coach called time-out, and she trotted over to the bench. Mrs. Klepp, her coach, patted her on her sweaty back and said, "Keep it up, Sammy. You're doing great." **87.** had been dating, had given, had wanted, had been making, had been surprised, had thought, had explained, had broken, had offered **88.** 1. *real* should be *really* 2. *good* should be *well*, *bad* should be *badly* 3. *strangely* should be *strange* 4. *real fast* should be *really quickly* 5. *well* should be *good* 6. *consistent* should be *consistently*, and *hardly* should be *hard* 7. *real bad* should be *really badly* 8. *good* should be *well* 9. *real* should be *really* 10. *fierce* should be *fiercely*, and *fairly* should be *fair*. **89.** Answers will vary. **90.** Answers will vary. **91.** Similes: as an alley cat, fierce as a tiger, like an angel Metaphors: His guitar spits fire, He's an umbrella in a rainstorm, Chicken soup for the flu. **92.** Answers will vary. **93.** Hyperbole: best basketball player ever to live, scores about a million points every game she plays, towers over all the other girls like a mountain over an ant hill, has been playing basketball for her whole life, she could feel Sammy bouncing a basketball in her womb, Sammy has eyes in the back of her head, She can see what her opponent is going to do even before she decides to do it, and she flies down the court like Superwoman. Similes/ metaphors: towers like a mountain over an anthill, flies like Superwoman **94.** Mrs. Klepp was a hair taller than Mr. Klepp; Mrs. Klepp wasn't quite as accomplished a dancer; dipped him very gently, inadvertently dropping him on his head **95.** Answers will vary. **96.** Excited: 1. His moustache twitched more. His eyes sparkled more. His dimples dimpled more. Worried: 1. He paced up and down the classroom. 2. He raked his hands through his hair. 3. He jingled his pocket change. Other answers will vary. **97.** ¶ Of course, as soon as Mr. Klepp admitted he was keeping secrets, his students began bothering him relentlessly to tell them. "If you tell us, we won't even

Daily Warm-Ups: Daily Edits

make you get a Mohawk at the end of the quarter if our grades go up," Sammy promised. ¶ "Speak for yourself," Cliff said, "but I do really want to know what's going on." (¶)"Look," Mr. Klepp explained, "I can't tell you one secret because I promised someone very special that I wouldn't. I can't tell you the other secret because I promised myself that I wouldn't. And I think you have to agree that I'm a special person, too." Mr. Klepp smiled smugly. **98.** *grieted* should be *greeted*, *releef* should be *relief*, *seeted* should be *seated*, *teecher* should be *teacher*, *Tomatoe* should be *Tomato*, *Potatoe* should be *Potato*, *cheared* should be *cheered*, *peece* should be *piece*, *beemed* should be *beamed*, *reed* should be *read*. **99.** Misspelled words are 1. tomato, blue 2. potato 3. bumpy, potato 4. tomato 5. heroes 6. skies 7. bright 8. hero, a lot 9. tomato 10. then, veto 11. witty, noble 12. lying, shoe **100.** You're Invited!
To: A baby shower for Mr. and Mrs. Klepp
When: February 28, 20__ at 2:30
Where: Mr. Klepp's classroom
Please bring the following items: five dollars for a gift, a baked good, and a picture of yourself as a baby. (It will be returned to you after the party.) **101.** 1. The cake, which took Sammy and Izzie three hours to bake, was delicious. 2. The boys photocopied all of the baby pictures that the students had brought to make a collage for the Klepps. 3. Mrs. Klepp, who is quite sentimental, cried when the students jumped out from behind the door and shouted, "Surprise!" 4. Mr. Klepp, whose father was a pastry chef, said the cake was the most delicious he had ever tasted. 5. The Klepps thanked their students, whom they really appreciated, for the party. **102.** 2. *where* should be *that* 2. *that* should be *which* 3. *kind* should be *kinds*, *said facts* should be changed to *they* 4. *some* should be *somewhat* 5. *then* should be *than* 6. *without* should be *unless*, *have* should be *had* 7. *ways* should be *way* 8. *there* should be eliminated **103.** In the springtime, Cliff's thoughts turn to business pursuits. When the grass begins to grow and the weeds come out, Cliff passes fliers out to all of his neighbors and reminds them of Cliff's Landscaping services. He also has a spring clean-up service, a babysitting service, and a petsitting service for people on vacation. When Cliff cleans out a garage, he does a thorough job of taking out the trash, scrubbing the area,

Daily Warm-Ups: Daily Edits

painting, and organizing the tools. Homeowners love to see their houses shine and sparkle after Cliff is done. Garden beds also look neat after his pruning and raking. Cliff's mom always wonders how a kid with such a messy room can do such a good job of cleaning and organizing other people's stuff. **104.** Answers will vary. **105.** Answers will vary. **106.** Answers will vary. **107.** Answers will vary. **108.** 1. Nate and Leo, both members of Pete's band, are in eighth grade. 2. Mr. Klepp, a published author, teaches language arts at CCMS. 3. Truck Stop, a student band, is playing at a Battle of the Bands. 4. Sammy and Izzie, two girls in Mr. Klepp's class, are starting a band, too. 5. Fiona, a girl who wants to join the band, plays the fiddle and sings beautifully. 6. Izzie and Sammy, the bandleaders, are not sure they want someone to join who will only live in town for a few more months. **109.** Here is one way to punctuate: Fiona was lying on her bed, trying not to let her host family hear her crying. She felt completely betrayed and, worst of all, it was her best American friends who had betrayed her! Because the Battle of the Bands was coming to Charlotte Cove, the girls wanted to start a group and try to win the $100 prize, but they were

also thinking of creating a band that would take the place of Truck Stop when some of the members went on to high school. She had asked them at lunchtime if she could join the band, which they had named the Charlottes, but they had told her they had to think about it. She had just gotten off Instant Messenger with them and, much to her astonishment, they had told her that they were going to ask their friend Mei to join the band instead. Fiona had nothing against Mei, a talented singer and guitarist in Mr. Abdul's class, but she didn't understand why she couldn't be in the band, too. What was wrong with her? She was a really good singer, and she knew her soprano voice would sound beautiful with Mei's alto. Her fiddle playing, which had won her several competitions in Scotland, would give the band a unique sound. Totally exasperated, she rolled over and tried to get some sleep. **110.** *You're* should be *your, click* should be *clique, scent* should be *sent, complementing* should be *complimenting, fare* should be *fair, fourth* should be *forth, recent* should be *resent, confidant* should be *confident, buy* should be *by, altar* should be *alter, allusion* should be *illusion,* and *effect* should be *affect.* **111.** Here's one possible revision: It was the end of the

Daily Warm-Ups: Daily Edits

quarter, and the students in Mr. Klepp's class were more excited than usual because they had worked harder that term than any other in their lives. They wanted to see Mr. Klepp get a Mohawk. In fact, Cliff had persuaded his dad, who was a barber, to go to school with him, just on the chance that the students had accomplished their goal of raising their class average by five points. Mr. Klepp decided to turn the report cards into a math game. Without putting up people's names, he wrote their second-quarter averages up next to their third-quarter scores. He asked students to add up all the second-quarter averages and divide by the number of students in the class. Then he asked them to do the same of the third-quarter column. Finally, he asked them to subtract the first column from the second column. The result was 5.2. The students howled with excitement. Mr. Klepp was getting a Mohawk! **112.** Answers will vary.
113. Misspelled words: *rhyme, grammar, Every, sensory, fancy, language, usually,* and *rhythm.* Check to see which of the statements students agreed with. **114.** Answers will vary. **115.** clang, boom, whine, roar **116.** Outlines will vary somewhat, but the paragraph is in spatial order.

117. Answers will vary. **118.** Pete was going out to dig bloodworms with his Uncle Gus, <u>and</u> he wasn't looking forward to the back-breaking work. <u>First</u>, he had to get up at 4:30 A.M. so that he could put in a full day and get to the flats before anyone else. <u>Next</u>, he had to put on huge hip waders, rubber boots that went all the way up his legs. He wore them right over his pajamas; there was no need to shower when he would be digging in salty muck all day. <u>After he had his legs covered</u>, he put on a thermal undershirt and three sweaters. <u>Outside all of those layers</u>, he wore a raincoat to keep the morning mist off his back. He knew that by midmorning, he would be tearing off the layers, but for now he wanted to be warm. <u>Finally</u>, he ate the big breakfast that his mom cooked him and waited for Uncle Gus's truck to arrive. The paragraph is in chronological order. **119.** Answers will vary.
120. Answers will vary. **121.** 1. The CCMS Lady Hawks went to the Girls' Basketball State Championship. 2. The girls were all nervous, but Sammy might have been the most nervous one on the team. 3. She had led the Lady Hawks to one of their best seasons ever, and she was only in the sixth grade. 4. She imagined playing on the

Daily Warm-Ups: Daily Edits

WNBA someday, perhaps for the New York Liberty. 5. As she played, she thought about the people in the crowd. 6. Maybe there was a scout from a great college team, such as the University of Connecticut. 7. Sammy was a little girl with dreams as big as the Washington Monument. **122.** It was the second half of the state championship between the Lady Hawks and their great rivals, the Richland Raiders. Coach Klepp, who was eight months pregnant, was walking up and down the sidelines nervously and shouting instructions to her girls. When Izzie made a sloppy pass to Fiona, Coach Klepp signaled time-out, and the girls huddled. "Izzie, we can't afford that kind of mistake," Mrs. Klepp said. "I know, Coach. I'm sorry," Izzie answered sadly. "That's okay, Izzie. Just be sure to look at each other." "And if you're open, speak up, right Coach?" Sammy said. "Absolutely, Captain," Mrs. Klepp replied. "Now who's going to win?" "We are!" the girls shouted. **123.** All of the moms and dads in the audience were wearing teal and black, the team colors for the Hawks. Some were holding signs that said, "Defense!" and "Fly High, Hawks!" Sammy's parents, George and Grace, had a sign of their own. It said, "Go Lucky 7!"

because that was Sammy's number. Usually, Grace, Sammy's mom, chatted with her friends when she went to games, but this time she was completely focused on the game. Sammy made a pass, and Grace shouted, "Good job, Chickadee!" which was her pet name for Sammy. George nudged his wife's shoulder and explained, "Gracie, star athletes aren't usually called Chickadee." **124.** The game was down to the last twenty-four seconds, and Fiona had the ball. The score was 101 to 102, and Fiona knew that the game depended on her. She thought about her options. She could pass the ball to Sammy, but she was double-teamed. She could pass the ball to Roxy, but she hadn't been shooting well lately. She could pass it to Izzie, the point guard, but, to be perfectly honest, she was still angry with Izzie. She couldn't forget that Izzie was the one who had said she couldn't be in the Charlottes, the band that the girls were putting together. She knew that shouldn't matter, but . . . "Fiona, I'm open!" Izzie shouted. Fiona looked at the clock: twelve seconds. She chest-passed to Izzie, who bounced the ball to Sammy, who somehow, miraculously, faked out her two guards and made a layup for the win! Fiona felt Izzy's and Sammy's

Daily Warm-Ups: Daily Edits

arms around her, and she realized she had made the right choice. **125.** Answers will vary. **126.** The girls in the locker room were screaming, laughing, and pouring sports drinks on each other. All of them were feeling like winners, and Fiona was no exception. But she couldn't help but notice that both Izzie and Sammy were getting more attention from the girls and even the coach than she was. Everybody was remembering that Izzie had assisted Sammy with the basket, but nobody was remembering that Fiona had assisted Izzie. Either Sammy or Izzie was calling Fiona's name. She looked over, and Sammy said, "Are you coming?" "Where?" Fiona asked. "We're having a victory party at my house," Sammy answered. "One of us must have told you, right?" "No," Fiona answered. "Nobody tells me anything. I can't go because my host family and Claire's cousin are taking me to dinner." "That's too bad," Sammy said, but Fiona wasn't sure she meant it. **127.** Images that students notice will vary. The description emphasizes visual information and doesn't mention sense of touch. Sense of taste (spicy as jambalaya) is only mentioned in a simile. **128.** Answers will vary. **129.** Answers will vary.

130. Answers will vary. **131.** Answers will vary. One option: 1. Because orchestra practice was before school at CCMS, Fiona always dreaded it. 2. She was from Scotland, where school started much later in the morning. 3. She thought she was going to have a bad day, until she saw Beau standing with an electric guitar in the strings section. 4. Although he obviously loved music, she hadn't expected him to be a "band geek." 5. After she screwed up her courage, she stood next to him and plugged her electric fiddle into his amp. **132.** 1. Beau wasn't surprised to see Fiona with a fiddle, because he knew that Celtic music was popular in the United Kingdom. 2. Fiona didn't know that fiddles were also popular in Cajun music, which Beau played. 3. Beau asked Fiona, who blushed furiously, to play a little bit of a Celtic song he knew before practice started. 4. When she played the song, tears came to Beau's eyes. OR Tears came to Beau's eyes when she played the song. 5. Fiona asked Beau to play her something, so he played her a bit of a zydeco song. **133.** Answers will vary. **134.** Answers will vary. **135.** Answers will vary. **136.** Sights: see the beautiful pattern cut into the green

Daily Warm-Ups: Daily Edits

grass of the diamond, see the streetlights sparkling on top of the Green Monster. Smells: cut grass, pretzels, hot dogs, and sunscreen. Sounds: crack of the bat and roar of faithful fans cheering. Tastes: nachos dripping with cheese, salty pretzels. Touch: fizzy sodas that tingle on my tongue. Misspelled words: *beautiful, stadium, including, hiatus, pretzels, mountains, eaten, nachos, tongue, diamond*.
137. Hyperbole: mountains stretch to infinity, midsummer days go on forever, a million grazing sheep, drive for days. Misspelled words: *Isle, Misty, mountains, shrouded, infinity, emerald, grazing, dirt, roads, traveler*.
138. Similes: Windows like big, sleepy eyes, porch as wide and comforting as my grandmother's lap, fragrance floats like music, mosquitoes as big as my ear, alligators as fierce as a bear defending its cub, steamier than a sauna, wilder than any jungle. Metaphors: Jasmine and honeysuckle wrap the house in a big embrace, house is paradise. Misspelled words: *shuttered, sleepy, porch, comforting, wrap, fragrance, through, mosquitoes, alligators, paradise*.
139. Examples of understatement: pretty puny, little picture gallery called the Louvre, which has a couple of relatively well-known works of art, pretty good-sized

market, nice selection. **140.** Answers will vary. **141.** Answers will vary. **142.** Answers will vary. **143.** The members of Truck Stop were getting worried. They had been the most popular band all year, but now they had a rival that was just as good as, if not better than, they were. Truck Stop was a good band, but their music was pretty conventional. They did a lot of covers of other people's music, and they mostly played songs that are heard on the radio. The Charlottes was a different kind of band. They played a multicultural mix of zydeco, Celtic, Afro-Caribbean, and punk music that nobody had ever heard before. **144.** Answers will vary, but students should eliminate Yo Moms and Dads; majorly important; dorky parents; I know, you probably think middle school bands are lame; cuz; Besides, without you guys; gig; So come, okay?; stick in your kid's backpack; or something, okay, cuz we really; Thanks a bunch. **145.** Answers will vary. **146.** Mr. Klepp was having difficulty making the students in his class pay attention to his lessons. He kept stating the same information over and over again, because nobody was paying attention. Instead, everybody was worrying about the upcoming Battle of the Bands. He

Daily Warm-Ups: Daily Edits

decided to bring in copies of his young adult novel to read to the class. Creating an imaginary world in fiction is a tricky job. Mr. Klepp had used qualities of his students in his fictional characters, and he was a bit worried that his students would feel betrayed about appearing in his book. Would they think the characters were likable? He decided that revealing the stories to the students ahead of time was the easiest solution. **147.** Answers will vary. **148.** Answers will vary. **149.** The lights came up on Fiona's band, and suddenly she was playing a song she had never heard before, called "Do You Want to Be a Failure?" She had expected to play "Punk Rhapsody," a song she and Beau had written together months ago. Why was she playing this new song instead of "Punk Rhapsody"? How was she supposed to know her part, when Beau had just shoved it under her nose and said, "Play this"? It was especially horrible because when she looked down at the music, Beau's face looked up at her and screamed, "Don't disappoint me!" Fiona awoke exhausted and embarrassed. Her dream had been fascinating, and it was somewhat humorous, now that she was awake. She immediately rolled over and went back to sleep, hoping that her

excitement about tomorrow wouldn't cause her any more bad dreams. **150.** Answers will vary. **151.** All the underlined words are palindromes, words or phrases that are spelled the same backwards. Every spring the sixth grade at CCMS took a trip to Camp Kutituk in the wilds of Maine. There, students learned to canoe and kayak, enjoyed listening to the peep of spring frogs, and savored the warm noon sun shining on their backs. When the kids arrived at the camp, their counselors, Ada, Bob, Otto, and a guy nicknamed Radar, were there to greet them. As soon as they had settled into their bunks, the counselors played a gag on them. Radar shouted, "Ready, aim, fire!" and they pulled out water balloons from behind their backs. The kids were at first terrified, but they laughed when they realized it was a joke. **152.** Students may notice that Fiona's date is written differently. American spellings are *gray, practice, colorful, savor, flavors, humorous, program*. **153.** Answers will vary. **154.** Answers will vary. **155.** On the bus ride home from Camp Kutituk, Mr. Klepp and the kids played a trivia game called "Stump the Chump." They had to quiz Mr. Klepp on his knowledge of rock music, books, and films.

Daily Warm-Ups: Daily Edits

"Okay, Mr. Klepp," Pete started. "Who sings, 'I Want to Be a Lifeguard'?" "That's easy," Mr. Klepp answered. "The B-52s. Who sings 'Stairway to Heaven'?" "Led Zeppelin, of course," Sammy said. "Even I knew that. What is the name of the movie starring John Travolta and Olivia Newton-John?" she asked. "Um, I think it's called *Fat*," Fiona said. Everybody laughed and Sammy explained, "No, it's *Grease*, silly!" "I've got one," Mr. Klepp said. "Does anyone know who wrote *War and Peace*?" "Is that a song?" Beau asked. "No, it's one of the great works of Russian literature, written by Leo Tolstoy." **156.** When the class got back from camp, their greenhouse garden was overflowing with fresh vegetables. Mrs. Klepp's class had taken care of LuLu, the class's goose, but nobody had weeded the garden. There were tomatoes so ripe that they bent their vines. Heads of lettuce were crowding each other out, and pea pods were bursting their seams. Carrots were poking their orange heads out of the ground, and magenta beets were swelling out of the ground. "Looks like it's time to harvest!" Mr. Klepp proclaimed when they got back to school. The kids spent their science class in the greenhouse, digging up the fruits of their labors.

157. The next day, neither Mr. Klepp nor Mrs. Klepp was in school. The class speculated about what might be going on. "Either Mrs. Klepp is having her baby, or they decided to give up teaching and join the circus," Pete guessed. The kids were disappointed that Mr. Klepp was gone, but they were excited to have a substitute, because they figured both the substitute and Mr. Klepp would not expect them to get real work done. What a surprise it was when their substitute, Dr. Bodwell, required them to memorize not only the Periodic Table of the Elements but also a Shakespearean sonnet! **158.** Dear Mr. Klepp: I'm glad you and Mrs. Klepp are finally having the baby, but I've got to tell you it's having a horrible effect on your class. We were all right the first day, but things just keep getting worse. Dr. Bodwell is so strict, he never gives us a break, and we have to do the most boring stuff. You wouldn't believe me if I told you. We spent approximately three days just doing grammar! We never get any peace and quiet from his nagging. I need your advice, Mr. Klepp. I've become much better behaved than I formerly was, but having this substitute is making me lose my mind! What can I do to keep my morale up and not end up at

Daily Warm-Ups: Daily Edits

the principal's office? Your desperate student, Cliff **159.** Konrad and Julie Klepp are proud to announce the birth of their daughter, Chloe McGraw Klepp. Chloe was born at Richland Hospital at 9:59 A.M. on April 30, 20__. She weighed 8 lbs. and 2 oz. Mother and daughter are both healthy and resting comfortably. Chloe's grand-parents are Konrad Klepp, Sr., and his wife Maria of Richland, and Reginald Grover and Louise McGraw of Ames, Iowa. Chloe also has seven aunts and uncles and twelve cousins on her father's side. **160.** Dear Konrad, Thank-you for entrusting me with your students. They were quite good, with a few exceptions. (See attached list.) During my time in your classroom, we studied grammar, chemistry, and creative writing. I have left folders of the students' work on your desk. I hope you have a marvelous time with your new baby. Fatherhood, as I'm sure you'll discover, is a wonderful experience. Yours truly, Bud Bodwell, PhD **161.** Every May, CCMS held elections for class officers and for student council representatives. There were six positions for each class: president, vice president, secretary, and treasurer, plus two student council representatives. Several students in Mr.

Klepp's class were planning to run. Either Sammy or Izzie was going to run for president, and the other one would run for vice president. Cliff, who had lots of experience working with money, was running for treasurer, and Pete was planning to run for student council representative. **162.** Welcome Prospective Class Officers and Representatives: Congratulations on your decision to run for elective office at CCMS. Participation in student-run government is both a duty and a privilege. Students elected by their peers have a great deal of responsibility. They must speak not only for themselves, but also for their fellow students. Don't be fearful about that burden, but don't take it too lightly, either. Run a decent campaign, treat your opponents with respect, and your classmates will respect you. Good luck to all. **163.** 1. Sammy and Izzie: An Administration for the Environment! 2. Clean up CCMS: Vote for Sammy and Izzie as President and Vice President 3. Do Things Differently: Vote for Sammy and Izzie 4. A Vote for Cliff is a Vote for Cash 5. Cliff is Really Funny; He'll Take Care of Your Money 6. Cliff: Responsible, Sensible, and Wise 7. Vote for Pete! He's a Good Listener 8. Pete

Daily Warm-Ups: Daily Edits

Rocks! Elect him for Your Representative 9. Vote Pete for Student Council. He'll Make Your Preferences Known! **164.** Answers will vary. Misspelled words: *trustworthy, favorites, collaborate, fund-raisers, class's* **165.** Answers will vary. Misspelled words: *Principal, environment, throw, Valuable, waste, produces, a lot, combat, environmental, raised, recycling* **166.** Answers will vary. Misspelled words: *communication, shoulder, lean, accomplishments, government* **167.** The time for campaigning had finally come to an end, and the students were voting. To celebrate the occasion, Mr. Klepp was wearing an Uncle Sam outfit, with a red and white striped hat and a fake beard. All of the kids had fought hard for their positions, and they had known from the beginning that some of them would have to lose. Still, they wished they could have all won. That afternoon, Ms. Perez, the principal, read the names of the winners over the intercom. Amazingly, all of the kids from Mr. Klepp's class who had run were winners. **168.** Answers will vary. **169.** The first job of the CCMS Student Council was to plan events for the end of the year. They had to prepare for the following events: Eighth-Grade Graduation, Step-Up Day for incoming sixth-graders, a final assembly, and Field Day. Claire, who only had a few weeks left as president before she moved up to high school, was in charge of events. She put students on committees: Pete was on the Field-Day team, Cliff was on the Step-Up Day group, Isabel was on the Graduation Committee, and Sammy was on the Assembly Committee. **170.** Field-Day Agenda

7:30–8:30 A.M.: Flag Football: Sixth Grade vs. Seventh Grade and Eighth Grade vs. Teachers
8:30–9:30 A.M.: Winner of Sixth/Seventh Grade vs. Winner of Eighth Grade/Teachers
9:30–10:00 A.M.: Three-Legged Race
10:00–11:00 A.M.: Pie Eating Contest
11:00 A.M.–12:00 P.M.: Outdoor Concert

171. Answers will vary. Misspelled words: *Graders', Graduation, Ceremony, Two, graduate* **172.** Dear Mum and Dad, I can't believe that I will be home in two weeks! Living in the United States has been fun; nonetheless, I want to get home to the familiar places and people I love so much. I know you want me to try to pack lightly; however, I have gotten so many wonderful presents and souvenirs here that I don't know if I will be able to cut

Daily Warm-Ups: Daily Edits

down any more than I already have. I'm sending some photos of the people in my class so that you'll finally be able to put names with faces. Beau, my boyfriend, is the one with the wild ginger hair. Love and kisses, Fiona **173.** Answers will vary. **174.** This summer I plan to ride in an airplane for the first time in my whole life! I am going to Florida to see my grandmother and grandfather. I love Grammie and Gramp, and I haven't seen either of them since they moved to the South last year. We used to be next-door neighbors, so I have missed them a lot. My favorite uncle, whose name is Jimmy, is coming with me, so I won't be alone. **175.** Answers will vary. Here is one possibility: As you know, I'm going back to bonnie Scotland in two short weeks' time. I feel as though I have been in Maine for a long time. I have nothing against this beautiful place, but I really want to get back to my family and friends. I have had a wonderful time with you and this class. You are great people, and when I return to Scotland, I will tell everybody I see how wonderful you've been to me. **176.** I burn badly when I go out in the sun,

so I'm going to stay in my room and practice my guitar for hours. I want to come back to school next year as the leader of the new Truck Stop, because if I don't take over, the band is going to be in real trouble. I'm hoping that Izzie, Sammy, and Beau will join with Chrissie and me to form a new group, because we're both too small without one another. I'm also excited about going to ball games with my dad, fishing (with lots of sunscreen on, of course), and riding my bike to Cliff's house. **177.** As you can imagine, I have a busy summer planned for myself this year. I'm going to three camps: Bowdoin College Music Camp, Hoops Basketball Camp, and overnight camp at Camp Kutituk. I also want to work on some plans I have for the recycling program at school. I'm thinking about working with the town, too, so that we can collect waste from area businesses and households. Of course, I will also spend plenty of time hanging out on the beach, so don't worry about me! **178.** Answers will vary. **179.** Answers will vary. **180.** Answers will vary.

Turn downtime into learning time!

For information on other titles in the

Daily Warm-Ups series,

visit our web site: walch.com